ON FIRE

Studies in Rhetoric/Communication
Thomas W. Benson, series editor

ON FIRE

Five Civil Rights Sit-Ins and the Rhetoric of Protest

Edited by
Sean Patrick O'Rourke &
Lesli K. Pace

THE UNIVERSITY OF
SOUTH CAROLINA PRESS

© 2021 University of South Carolina
Sean Patrick O'Rourke, "Reading Bodies, Reading Books" © 2020 University of
 South Carolina
Stephen Schneider, "Nothing New for Easter" © 2020 University of South Carolina

Published by the University of South Carolina Press
Columbia, South Carolina 29208

www.uscpress.com

Manufactured in the United States of America

30 29 28 27 26 25 24 23 22 21
10 9 8 7 6 5 4 3 2 1

Library of Congress Cataloging-in-Publication Data
can be found at http://catalog.loc.gov/.

ISBN 978-1-64336-161-1 (paperback)
ISBN 978-1-64336-162-8 (ebook)

To our children:
  Tierney O'Rourke
  Lili and Ian Pace McDonald

"This world demands the qualities of youth: not a time of life but a state of mind, a temper of the will, a quality of the imagination, a predominance of courage over timidity, of the appetite for adventure over the love of ease."

  —Robert F. Kennedy
  "Affirmation Day" Address
  Cape Town, South Africa
  6 June 1966

Contents

Series Editor's Preface

In *On Fire: Five Civil Rights Sit-Ins and the Rhetoric of Protest,* editors Sean Patrick O'Rourke and Lesli K. Pace bring together a group of scholars to investigate the rhetorical structure of the Southern student lunch counter sit-ins of 1960. The resulting account of sit-ins and their variations through American history and across the American landscape, especially in the Jim Crow South, celebrates the courage, decency, and rhetorical acuity of the movement leaders and participants, against the backdrop of stubborn hatreds and habits of exclusion and exploitation, the recurring sin of American racism. O'Rourke, to take one small example, finds in the 1958 Code of Greenville, South Carolina, a requirement that public eating establishments maintain separate sets of dishes and utensils for Black and White customers and that "a separate facility shall be maintained and used for the cleaning of eating utensils and dishes furnished the two races." The hateful delicacy and rotten purity of such practices were made visible and untenable when well-dressed, young Black customers, with modest courtesy and loving courage, simply sat at White lunch counters and ordered a Coke. The actions of the college students who participated in those sit-ins were hardly protests at all but simply the enactment of ordinary, everyday shopping; they were protests only in context of the opposition with which they were met and not in the form that they presented in their enactment, and yet they are central to the history of American social protest and nonviolent direct action. The essays in this book help to illuminate the design, context, and development of the sit-ins as a rhetorical practice and open the way to ongoing work.

Thomas W. Benson
Series Editor

Acknowledgments

We thank the wonderful staff of the University of South Carolina Press, who could not have been more supportive. We give special thanks to Aurora Bell and Richard Brown, who helped conceive the idea for this volume and saw it through to completion. We also acknowledge our sincere appreciation and respect for one another, as well as note the value we place on our friendship even in the face of the most challenging aspects of this scholarly endeavor. We owe much to our families, especially Tierney O'Rourke, Jamie Capuzza, Mike McDonald, and Lili and Ian Pace McDonald. Sean also thanks his Sewanee colleagues, Melody Lehn, Terry Papillon, and Liesl Allingham; and Lesli thanks her University of Louisiana, Monroe colleagues, C. Turner Steckline Wilson, Mara Loeb, and Ruth Smith, for their good cheer, unflagging support, continued friendship, and unwavering encouragement. We thank Sewanee: The University of the South's Faculty Research Grants Committee, which provided funding in a time of fiscal uncertainty, for completion of the manuscript, and Camille Stallings, for her superb work on the index. Finally, we thank Adam Hawkins at Sewanee for his considerable help with the manuscript at various stages of the project.

INTRODUCTION

Five Civil Rights Sit-Ins and the Rhetoric of Protest

Sean Patrick O'Rourke & Lesli K. Pace

The social, political, and legal struggles that made up the larger civil rights movement of the mid-twentieth century produced and refined a wide range of rhetorical strategies and tactics. From letters, pamphlets, and newspaper ads to speeches, legal arguments, marches, and boycotts, civil rights activists and their opponents displayed, in fierce and brutal battle, an astounding rhetorical inventiveness. Arguably the most astonishing and certainly the least understood are the sit-in protests that swept the nation at the beginning of the 1960s. This book focuses tightly on five civil rights sit-ins of 1960 (in Greenville and Rock Hill, South Carolina; Louisville, Kentucky; Charlotte, North Carolina; and New Orleans, Louisiana) and is designed for students of rhetoric, protest, and sociopolitical movements, as well as those interested in American, African American, and Southern studies.

On Fire grows out of our larger work, *Like Wildfire: The Rhetoric of the Civil Rights Sit-Ins*. The earlier and lengthier book divides the sit-ins into three eras (protests before the February 1, 1960 Greensboro, North Carolina, sit-ins; sit-ins that spread "like wildfire"[1] just after Greensboro; and the lingering legacy found in more recent public activism and memory studies), and in each section our contributors focus on the distinctive rhetorical dimensions of particular protests as they emerged and responded to the demands of the cities and towns they sought to desegregate. Similarly, the contributors to the present work, *On Fire*, also study the sit-ins as markedly rhetorical activities. They suggest not only that the sit-ins were essentially persuasive conflicts in which participants invented and deployed arguments and actions in attempts to change segregated communities and the attitudes, traditions, and policies that maintained segregation but also that each community was different, sometimes dramatically so. These two aspects, the inherently rhetorical nature of the sit-ins and that each sit-in emerged from radically different local circumstances, makes studying the sit-in movement as challenging as it is rewarding. On the one hand it was a movement, with trajectories that can be charted and appreciated, leaders and cross-protest influences that can be identified, and striking similarities across individual disputes in a wide variety of cities and towns. On the other hand each community's sit-ins grew out of a specific, local *terroir*, and that complex of contexts—historical, cultural, economic, religious, and legal—gave to each sit-in protest a distinctive taste, none quite like any other.

Perhaps this explains why scholarship on the sit-in movement has advanced as it has, in fits and starts and almost always piecemeal, one or at best a few fragments at a time.[2] The traditional narrative of the sit-in movement—that it burst spontaneously into life on February 1, 1960, in Greensboro and died out sometime in 1964—serves as a poor frame to the movement. Its beginnings are deeper and more complex, and its breadth has yet to be fully measured.

As Blair Kelley has shown, the deepest sit-in roots extend back to the antebellum period, when African Americans resisted segregated trains, streetcars, and ferries in Massachusetts and New York. There, Frederick Douglass, Sarah Adams, Elizabeth Jennings, her father Thomas L. Jennings, the Reverend James W. C. Pennington, and the Legal Rights Association chose to protest segregated streetcars not by boycotting but by riding—by *sitting in* segregated cars until they were pulled out of their seats and, sometimes, thrown forcefully from the train. The sit-ins had mixed results: New England rail cars were eventually desegregated, and in New York Elizabeth Jennings sued for damages after being dragged from a car in 1854 and won. The protesters lost other cases.[3] But they established, over the course of their protests, both an effective method—sitting in—and a precedent of resistance.

Sit-ins were also prevalent in the postbellum period, especially during Reconstruction. Once again, the targets were streetcars and similar forms of public transportation. In March of 1867, African Americans in Charleston, South Carolina, began sitting in the city's new streetcars and by May had won legal access to them. In June, the military commander of the town extended those rights to railroads and steamboats.[4] That same May, newly freed Anglicized African Americans and mixed-race Francophone Afro-Creoles joined forces to overthrow New Orleans, Louisiana's "star-car" system in which Black riders were forced to ride in separate cars set aside for them.[5] Similar streetcar sit-ins took place in Richmond, Virginia (1867), and Louisville, Kentucky (1870–71).[6] In many of these protests, especially those that lasted for weeks and months, protesters used a combination of tactics, adding boycotts, legal actions, speeches, and demonstrations to their sit-in campaigns.

The Jim Crow era, especially the period after the Supreme Court's "separate but equal" interpretation of the 14th Amendment in *Plessy v. Ferguson*, presented

African Americans with new and virulent rules and rituals of segregation.[7] In this period, as Kelley and, before her, August Meier and Elliott Rudwick have shown, resistance more often took the form of boycotts rather than sit-ins, again with mixed results.[8] This period also saw the rise of new organizations—the Niagara Movement in 1905, reformed in 1909 as the National Association for the Advancement of Colored People (NAACP), and the Congress of Racial Equality (CORE) in 1942. It also revealed the changed conditions of the Great Depression sandwiched between two world wars, all wrapped in the Great Migration of six million African Americans from the South to the Northeast, Midwest, and West.[9] These changed conditions shaped the resistance and response of the time, providing new demands (and opportunities) for sit-in protests.

The arc of sit-ins from the Great Depression to Greensboro is not fully known. It runs, however, from Eleanor Roosevelt's 1938 "sit-between" in Birmingham, Alabama, to the 1939 sit-ins at Alexandria, Virginia's public library and New York's Shack Sandwich Shops; the Little Palace sit-in by Howard University students between 1942 and 1944; CORE's sit-in at Jack Spratt's in Chicago in 1943; the CIO sit-in in Columbus, Ohio, in 1947; and Des Moines, Iowa's Katz Drugs and St. Louis's Stix, Baer, & Fuller Department Store sit-ins of 1948.[10] Later, protesters staged sit-ins in Washington, DC, at Thompson's Restaurant from 1950 to 1953; in Baltimore, Maryland, at Read's Drugs (1955); in Durham, North Carolina, at the Royal Ice Cream Parlor (1957); in Wichita, Kansas, at Dockum Drugs (1958); in Oklahoma City at Katz Drugs (1958); and in Miami, Florida (1959),[11] just months before the Greensboro sit-ins of February 1, 1960. Given this arc, it is certainly fair to say that the 1960 sit-ins burst into flame not spontaneously but rather from the slow and steady fanning of many tiny sparks.

While not the "beginning" in any real sense then, Greensboro's sit-ins, unlike those before, ignited something unpredicted and unprecedented. Greensboro fired not only James Lawson and his Nashville students[12] but also, in such rapid succession that we lack exact numbers, students across North Carolina, then those in Virginia, South Carolina, Tennessee, Maryland, Kentucky, Alabama, and beyond. With the mid-April wade-ins to desegregate Mississippi's beaches, the movement had reached every state in the South.[13]

Estimates of sit-in activism in the period range from 50,000[14] to 70,000 participants in at least 150 communities across all the Southern states.[15] Participants were predominantly young, high school and college students, and often new to direct-action protest. Their sudden activity, as Lynne Olson makes clear, "caught the country completely by surprise." She suggests that

American college students, for the most part, were seen as politically apathetic, interested more in the material trappings of success than in changing the world. That was as true for black students as for white, with most black schools encouraging their students to conform to the values of white society, to aspire to middle-class respectability. Many African-American students in the late 1950s and early 1960s represented the first generation of their families to go to college, and their attendance often came as a result of great sacrifice by their parents. Theirs was a generation with the potential to become doctors and lawyers and professors, so when they sat in at local lunch counters, when they risked arrest and expulsion from school, they were also putting their futures at risk—the futures in which their parents had invested so much.[16]

Throughout the first year of the sit-in movement, students added considerably to the twin themes of sacrifice and risk: Their determination, perseverance, and endurance was frequently noted in the regional and national press, and their stoicism and general (though not universal) commitment to nonviolence gained them important though distant allies.[17]

The essays in this book offer close looks at five civil rights sit-ins of this early period. Sean Patrick O'Rourke directs attention to a little-known sit-in in Greenville, South Carolina, to reveal the importance of rhetorical somatics and visual imagery to the movement while deepening our understanding of the ways in which specific local conditions brought forth unique responses rhetorically adapted to those conditions. Stephen Schneider considers the "bodily rhetoric" of Louisville, Kentucky's "Nothing New for Easter" campaign to illustrate how that discourse created collective action frames of justice, identity, and agency. Richard W. Leeman contrasts the violence of the Rock Hill, South Carolina, sit-ins with the relatively peaceful Charlotte, North Carolina, protests. Using the lens of constitutive rhetoric, Leeman explains the importance of common rhetorical ground in protest reception and racial conflict resolution. Lesli K. Pace focuses on the visual imagery of the New Orleans sit-ins and, by combining notions of Christian rhetoric and *kairos*, demonstrates how just a few photographs created a story arc unique to New Orleans.

Our efforts with this project, now two books deep, have been to open the sit-ins to renewed inquiry. In particular, our hope is that *Like Wildfire* and *On Fire* will serve as catalysts for a new generation of scholars to expand our knowledge of the sit-ins by studying known sit-ins that have not yet been the subject of inquiry, discovering sit-in protests that have not yet been noticed in the scholarly literature, and charting the spread of sit-in protests and the social networks, organizational structures, and news media that fostered their growth.[18] We also hope this new generation of researchers will continue to flesh out the rhetorical strategies and tactics at work in the sit-in protests they investigate, the dynamic interplay between and among different rhetorical efforts, the limits of "sitting in," and the ways in which the sit-ins of 1960 foreshadow and inform today's protests.[19]

Notes

1. Farber and Bailey, *The Columbia Guide to America in the 1960s*, 16.

2. The four books on the sit-in movement generally (Oppenheimer's *The Sit-In Movement of 1960;* Morgan and Davies's edited collection, *From Sit-Ins to SNCC;* Schmidt's *The Sit-Ins;* and our own *Like Wildfire*) confirm the importance of considering the unique pieces of the movement while also attending to the common features that unite them. In addition to these works, other studies include, e.g., Bayor, "Atlanta, Georgia, 1960–1961" (briefly sketching the events and timeline of the Atlanta movement); Fleming, "White Lunch Counters and Black Consciousness" (connecting the Knoxville sit-ins to the emerging conceptions of Black consciousness); Garrow, *Atlanta, Georgia, 1960–1961* (setting Atlanta's sit-ins in that city's larger student movement); Graves, "The Right to be Served" (describing Oklahoma City's tumultuous sit-ins); Rodney L. Hurst, *It Was Never about a Hot Dog and a Coke!* (a memoir of the author's civil rights activities in Jacksonville, FL); Raymond A. Mohl, "South of the South" and "Interracial Activism" (considering the Miami sit-ins of 1959 as part of Miami's larger intercultural civil rights movement); O'Brien, *We Shall Not Be Moved* (situating the Jackson, Mississippi, sit-ins within the larger Mississippi struggle); Proudfoot, *Diary of a Sit-In* (providing firsthand impressions of the Greensboro sit-ins); Seals, "The Wiley-Bishop Student Movement" (detailing the March 1960 sit-ins in Marshall, Texas).

3. Kelley, *Right to Ride*, 15–32.

4. Hine, "The 1867 Charleston Streetcar Sit-Ins."

5. Fischer, "A Pioneer Protest."

6. For the beginnings of the Richmond protest, see Regnault, "Indictment of Christopher Jones." On Louisville, see Norris, "An Early Instance of Non-Violence."

7. *Plessy v. Ferguson*, 163 U.S. 537 (1896).

8. See, e.g., "Negro Boycotts of Segregated Streetcars in Virginia" and, more generally, Meier, *Negro Thought in America, 1880–1915*.

9. On the importance of these changes, see especially, Wilkerson, *The Warmth of Other Suns*.

10. For a good analysis of Roosevelt in Birmingham, see Lehn, "Liminal Protest." On the Alexandria sit-ins, see, e.g., Sullivan, "Lawyer Samuel Tucker." For New York, see "Divine's Followers Give Aid to Strikers." For the Little Palace, see Molina, "Our Boys, Our Bonds, Our Brothers," and Bynum, *NAACP Youth*, 39–40. For Chicago, see Grossman, "The Birth of the Sit-In." For Columbus, see "CIO Delegates" and "CIO Group." For Iowa and St. Louis, see Lawrence, "Since It Is My Right," and Phillips, "Lunch Counters and the Public Sphere," respectively.

11. On DC's Thompson's Restaurant, see Quigley, "How D.C. Ended Segregation." On Baltimore's Read's Drugs, see Cassie, "And Service for All." On Durham's Royal Ice Cream, see Gallagher, Zagacki, and Swift, "From 'Dead Wrong' to Civil Rights History." On Wichita's Dockum Drug Store sit-ins, see Eick, *Dissent in Wichita*. On Oklahoma City's Katz Drugs, see Devona Walker, "50 Years Ago, Children Helped Change Nation." For Miami, see "Close Counter Rather Than Serve Negroes."

12. Hoover, "The Nashville Sit-Ins."

13. On this succession, see especially Carson, *In Struggle*, 9–11.

14. See Lewis, *The Shadows of Youth*, 65; Olson, *Freedom's Daughters*, 147. See also, Southern Regional Council, "Special Report."

15. Farber and Bailey, *The Columbia Guide to America in the 60s*, 16; Fairclough, *Better Day Coming*, 242.

16. Olson, *Freedom's Daughters*, 147–48. But compare Chafe, *Civilities and Civil Rights*, 98 (arguing that the Greensboro sit-in was a "dramatic extension of, rather than a departure from, traditional patterns of Black activism in Greensboro").

17. See, e.g., Sitton, "Negro Sitdowns Stir Fear"; Halberstam, "A Good City Gone Ugly"; and Salisbury, "Fear and Hatred Grip Birmingham."

18. Consider, e.g., Andrews and Biggs, "The Dynamics of Protest Diffusion."

19. On the limits, see Varda, "Sit-In as Argument and the Perils of Misuse," 132–51.

READING BODIES, READING BOOKS

A Rhetorical History of the 1960
Greenville, South Carolina, Sit-Ins

Sean Patrick O'Rourke

Many of the sit-ins that occurred after the Greensboro, North Carolina, protests of February 1, 1960, followed the pattern of college students targeting segregated lunch counters. Always and everywhere at considerable risk when protesting segregation, college students, especially those studying away from home, nonetheless risked fewer reprisals against family members when they protested. And lunch counters were, after all, some of the most visible sites of segregation, for they highlighted the egregious inequities of the system: Black customers were welcome to shop in the store but were not allowed to dine with other customers. Shopping, it seemed, was impersonal (and profitable) enough to tolerate a Black presence, but the communal act of breaking bread was too intimate, too tied to friendship and family and home, to be done together. Black people who wanted to eat out were required to do so "out back," away from White customers and public scrutiny.

In Greenville, South Carolina, however, the pattern did not hold. The sit-in movement there began with ministers and high school students and focused its initial attention on the public airport and library, gradually expanding to include lunch counters, churches, swimming pools, skating rinks, and more. It was the result of a combined, multigenerational effort of students and teachers, congregants and ministers, protesters and lawyers, and reporters and photographers. Greenville's sit-in movement traced a dynamic, multifaceted rhetorical trajectory, one that arced across nearly three years and moved against a long-standing culture—with all that the term implies—of segregated cohabitation.

To say that it was multifaceted is to suggest that a protest movement, like a rhetorical text, can exhibit what Edwin Black some years ago called "prismatic" qualities,[1] offering those who engage it a complex, many-sided, multimodal persuasive appeal, a type of appeal long recognized as a central characteristic of rhetoric in controversy.[2] In practice and over time, a movement provides a *multiplex ratio*—a constellation of many reasons—for change, and the "reasons" proffered to desegregate Greenville were both verbal and kinetic: traditional speech and somatic rhetoric. To say that the movement had a "rhetorical trajectory" is to suggest that the Greenville sit-in movement is open to study from the perspective of rhetorical history generally[3] and as a complex of strategic rhetorical adaptations over time to "a series of rhetorical problems," fluid, multiple, and mutable "situations that call[ed] for public persuasion to advance a cause or overcome an impasse" more specifically.[4] Examining the rhetorical trajectory of the Greenville sit-ins by attending to the prismatic qualities of the movement reveals that it was no mere copycat protest but rather an organic, homegrown rhetorical movement in constant, considered flux as it adapted to changing conditions over the course of its existence.

I begin by considering Greenville's culture of segregation as the 1950s became the 1960s, with special attention to the physical and rhetorical construction of an apartheid city under the guise of harmony. I then look at four phases of the movement: the initial march and stand-in at the airport on the first day of 1960, the library sit-ins of March and July of that same year, the expansion of protests to lunch counters, churches, swimming pools, and skating rinks as the movement developed, and finally the culmination of protest efforts in the courts. I conclude with a few thoughts on Greenville's sit-in movement and some larger issues the study raises.

Greenville's Culture of Segregation

Greenville, the third-largest metropolitan area in South Carolina, is an old textile town located in the Upstate, fifty-five miles south of the North Carolina border, now on the I-85 corridor and Amtrak line between Atlanta and Charlotte. In the wake of the Supreme Court's decisions in *Brown v. Board of Education* (consolidating four separate cases, one of which, *Briggs v. Elliott,* was on appeal from South Carolina),[5] *Life* magazine ran a series of articles on race relations in five southern cities. Greenville was featured in the September 17, 1956, issue, in which Mayor Kenneth Cass claimed that "there's always been a good feeling in the race situation" in Greenville and predicted that the good relations between Black and White people would remain unless an outside agitator "comes in and stirs it up."[6] The truth, however, was that these three themes, good relations, minimal local discontent, and outside agitation, were a thin veneer, a stable and useful cover of what was, physically and rhetorically, a thoroughly segregated city.

Like other southern cities in 1959, Greenville was still physically segregated in almost every conceivable way. Public transportation, swimming pools, skating rinks, bathrooms, drinking fountains, libraries, and schools were all segregated by race, as were the lunch counters on Main (and every other) Street and the waiting rooms in the bus and train stations. Even institutions founded and nurtured by the Black community—such as the Phillis Wheatley Association, a community center founded in 1919, and the Sterling Industrial School, a "Negro" school founded in 1902—were eventually taken over by the White establishment and, ironically in light of today's dominant southern political ideology, converted from private centers of Black empowerment to White-controlled public or quasi-public institutions.[7]

Segregation was rigorously enforced by city, county, and state law enforcement officials and, equally important, by a structure of extralegal organizations. Most notorious of these was the Ku Klux Klan. Organized regionally just after the Civil War, the KKK terrorized Black citizens—especially Black voters—during Reconstruction but disbanded in the 1870s, only to rise for a "second coming" in the 1920s.[8] In Upstate South Carolina, the KKK was especially strong, often "aiding" police in their investigations and aggressively and sometimes brutally opposing labor organizers, voter registration drives, and individual Black citizens it thought posed a danger.[9] The threat and reality of physical violence was a fact of life for Black citizens of Greenville in the middle of the twentieth century. The city saw five lynchings between 1905 and 1933, and the 1947 lynching of Willie Earle received international notoriety.[10]

In many ways more powerful than the KKK, South Carolina's version of the White Citizens' Council, the South Carolina Segregation Committee (known informally as the Gressette Committee after the group's chair, Marion Gressette), sought to lead and control the effort to maintain segregation. Comprising White business, civic, and political leaders from across the state, the Gressette Committee warned, as Steve O'Neill has noted, of the bad press the KKK could give to segregation and sought to maintain the long-standing culture of segregated cohabitation by putting a professional face on it, one that spoke of racial harmony, prosperity, and cooperation.[11]

Greenville's physical segregation was buttressed by a more nuanced rhetorical segregation. The rhetoric of segregation drew upon debunked scientific theories of racial inferiority, Jim Crow–era constitutional interpretations of the Fourteenth Amendment, and fundamentalist readings of the Bible to propagate an "intellectual" opposition to desegregation. This rhetoric was potent and pervasive.[12]

The South produced a series of books in the mid-twentieth century that, taken together, perpetrated this cult of segregation. The more anthropological of these were only one small step removed from their intellectual forebears, works such as Samuel Morton's *Crania Americana* (1839) and Samuel Cartwright's "Diseases and Peculiarities of the Negro Race" (1851).[13] In their popular books, Stuart Landry (1945) and Theodore Bilbo (1946) refurbished these antebellum racial theories to stress the intellectual and ethical inferiority of Blacks for a New South eager to continue to justify segregation.[14] Similarly Tom Brady's *Black Monday* (1955)[15] and the congressional "Southern Manifesto" (1956) used the constitutional theories of the Jim Crow era to attack the Supreme Court's 1954 *Brown* decision as unwarranted judicial activism at best and social engineering wrapped in a judicial coup at worst.[16]

This segregationist thought was aggressively supported and disseminated by local Greenville media, especially the rhetorical efforts of Wayne C. Freeman and William D. Workman Jr. of the *Greenville News.* Freeman was editor of the *News* and served as an officer of the Gressette Committee. Over the course of several years, he wrote editorials defending segregation "as morally right, legally right, and necessary for the preservation of peace and good order."[17] Workman was the *News*'s political correspondent in Columbia, who also wrote for Charleston's *Post and Courier* and Columbia's *The State* and who published the segregationist *The Case for the South* in 1960.[18] Their efforts served to embed the themes of good relations, minimal local discontent, and outside agitation into the media's coverage of civil rights protests and to wrap them in what Jennifer E. M. Hill has identified as a frame of "victimage"—the notion that somehow the South was a victim of the slander, discrimination, and violence of northern integrationists and their southern stooges.[19]

The secular media, however, were not alone. Equally powerful were the voices of the fundamentalist Protestant churches and schools. Known locally as the "Buckle of the Bible Belt," Greenville boasted numerous Christian churches in 1959 and had become home to Bob Jones University in 1947 and nearby North Greenville Junior College in 1950, two conservative Christian universities. Conservative White ministers preached a gospel of segregation, rooting their views in Old and New Testament accounts of slavery, race, and Christian duty. Perhaps most influential of these was Bob Jones, founder of the university bearing his name. On April 17, 1960, he delivered a radio address titled "Is Segregation Scriptural?" and published a pamphlet version of it shortly thereafter.[20] Speaking to and for "Bible-believing Christians," Jones argued forcefully in favor of segregation just after the Greenville sit-in movement had begun in earnest. In strikingly contradictory terms, Jones acknowledged that "no race is inferior in the will of God" and yet claimed that segregation was God's "established order" and that desegregation, an effort to "run over God's plan and God's established order," would cause only "trouble."[21] Similar arguments are evident in the contemporaneous *Essays on Segregation,* a slim volume of seven essays by White, southern Protestant preachers, including four from the Carolinas.[22]

The culture of segregation presented civil rights activists with enormous challenges. That culture said that segregation led to good relations and minimal discontent, while desegregation was evidence of outside agitation. Segregation was law and order; desegregation was illegal disruption of that order. Segregation was natural and scientifically justified; desegregation went against science and the natural order. Segregation was Christian for it was God's will; desegregation was unchristian and defied God's will. And in 1959 defiance of that culture brought punishment: lynchings were well within living memory, and protesters bucking the segregationist White power structure in the Cold War–era South risked loss of jobs, denial of credit, and the noxious labels of "communist" and "socialist."[23] Opposing the segregated South was dangerous business, and civil rights advocates therefore had to invent rhetorical strategies that countered the racist claims of intellectual and ethical inferiority, placed them and not segregationists on the side of good relations, made segregationists instigators of local discontent, and contrasted Black Christian virtue with White Christian hypocrisy.[24]

Ministers at the Airport

"Beginnings" are usually elusive, of course, but Greenville's public civil rights protests began on January 1, 1960, and focused on the city's segregated public facilities.[25] They were prompted by the arrival of two visitors in February and October 1959. The February visitor was Richard Henry, a civilian Air Force employee from Michigan who sought to fly out of Greenville's downtown airport. When he entered the airport, he was told that he had to sit in the "Negro" waiting room, a room less comfortable and more poorly appointed than the "White" waiting room. When Henry complained, he was told he could fly out of another airport if he wanted to. Henry filed complaints with the U.S. Air Force, the national NAACP, and local airport authorities. With the help of the NAACP Legal Defense fund, he filed suit in federal court, claiming discrimination and denial of the equal protection of law guaranteed by the Fourteenth Amendment.[26] Little was done locally, however, before the second visitor arrived in October.

On October 25, 1959, as Henry's case was making its way through the federal court system, Jackie Robinson, Major League Baseball's first Black player, flew into Greenville to address a meeting of the South Carolina NAACP. A small group including Robinson's colleague Gloster Current and local Black leaders Willie T. Smith Jr., Rev. H. P. Sharper, and Billie Fleming waited to greet him. They were told to leave the White waiting room. Later that day Robinson returned to the airport to fly home, and once again he and his companions (among them the Reverend and Mrs. James S. Hall) were harassed by airport officials and threatened with arrest. This time, however, Robinson was accompanied by a contingent of Greenville's most prominent Black civic leaders, including the local NAACP president, several ministers, and at least one lawyer. Robinson himself was well connected, and he fired off two letters to Thurgood Marshall, urging the NAACP Legal Defense team to take action.[27]

Marshall refused on the grounds that the issue was already in the courts (Richard Henry's case) and another action would be redundant and therefore a waste of limited resources. For the local Black community, Greenville's segregated municipal airport had long been a sore spot. All too often national and international visitors' first impression of their community was of the airport's segregated waiting rooms, visible reminders of Greenville's flagrant disregard for the Supreme Court's 1954 declaration that "separate is inherently unequal" and the Court's 1955 order to desegregate with "all deliberate speed." Such contempt was all the more maddening because the U.S. Constitution gives the federal government, not state or local officials, clear authority over interstate commerce.[28] Embarrassed by the Robinson incident and upset by the lack of progress, Greenville's Black leaders decided to act. They organized a protest march and prayer vigil on Emancipation Day, January 1, 1960.

In Greenville it was the pebble that started an avalanche, the trickle that became a flood. The march and prayer vigil were the first organized, overtly public acts of Greenville's civil rights movement. Organizers and participants indicate that the march included between 1,000 and 1,500 marchers, who drove cars and then trudged in a bitingly cold, icy sleet and rain from Springfield Baptist Church downtown out to the airport.[29] The Reverend Hall called their march a "prayer pilgrimage." Outside the terminal the group sang "America" as fifteen of them, led by Hall, entered the airport. The Reverend H. P. Sharper of Florence asked for blessings on "our friends" and "mercy on our enemies" and prayed "that history might be made here." The Reverend Matthew D. Mc-Cullough of Orangeburg read a five-point resolution condemning "the stigma, the inconvenience, and the stupidity of racial segregation," a system that made Blacks "second-class citizens." He urged that no one should acquiesce to the "degradations" of "Southern tradition" or be satisfied with the mere "crumbs of citizenship." The resolution characterized the march as "an expression of patriotism" and declared that "with faith in this nation and its God we shall not relent, we shall not rest, we shall not compromise, we shall not be satisfied until every vestige of racial discrimination and segregation has been eliminated from all aspects of public life."[30]

A close reading of the words of the airport protest indicates a keen attentiveness to the dynamics of Greenville's culture of segregation. The singing of Rev.

Samuel F. Smith's "America," one of the oldest hymns in the American songbook and one that, in the 1950s, was considered less edgy than Woody Guthrie's "This Land Is Your Land," invited listeners to see the protest less as a radical event and more as an attempt to reclaim a right due to all Americans. The description of the event as a "prayer pilgrimage" and the opening Christian prayer inoculated against charges of anti-Christian protest, and the call for "blessings" and "mercies" countered the good relations trope of segregationist rhetoric. Reverend McCullough's five-point resolution, while strongly worded, mediated against the presumption of intellectual and ethical inferiority by its calls for citizenship, patriotism, and the best in southern traditions; its elegant language; and its anaphoristic power. And while the protest most certainly evidenced discontent, all participants were long-time South Carolinians and in no way outside agitators.

The words, however, were only a part of the protest. When protests are at least in part nonverbal, as is the case with marches and sit-ins, they become instances of rhetorical somatics, the rhetorical use not of words but of the very bodies of the protesters.[31] Protestors place their bodies where they are not supposed to be and, through this juxtaposition of Black bodies in "White" places, offer a vision of a new, different, desegregated South. In the Greenville Airport march, the protesters used their bodies to deploy the visual rhetorical figure of *enargia,* the generic name for a family of figures devoted to vivid description, figures that lend themselves to the visualization of places, faces, characters, and actions. Two figures in this family, *chronographia* and *pragmatographia,* were particularly important, for they functioned to represent vividly certain historical or recurring time and the action within it (waiting time or traveling time) to depict a different reality—Black travelers waiting where and when they wanted to.

The images of the stand-in reinforced the words of the protest. All fifteen who entered the airport were members of the Black middle class—professionals, mainly ministers—and defied in every way the negative images of Black Americans evoked by segregationist rhetors such as Landry, Bilbo, and Brady. Their presence in the airport terminal caused no disruption of service, no "trouble," and reinforced the idea that good relations in Greenville did not depend on segregation.

As is the case with any form of rhetorical argument, however, these claims could be contested. Because the argument was verbal and visual, the newspapers used reports with photographic texts to deflect the thrust of the argument and to suggest a different set of conclusions. In one sense the newspapers deployed the same figures but created narratives that supported their versions of protest.

The morning paper, the *Greenville News,* ran a brief article announcing the intended demonstration in its January 1 edition. The article noted the scheduled time of the march as well as the leaders associated with it, Rev. Hall of the Congress of Racial Equality and Rev. T. B. Thomas, president of the Greenville Ministerial Alliance, which the paper called the "Greenville (Negro) Ministerial Alliance."[32] The next day the *News*'s description of the march invited readers to consider the protest as less threatening and less important than it clearly was. Downplaying the numbers, the *News* claimed that "about 250" participated in the march on the airport, an estimate that was a quarter of the most conservative estimate of those involved in the march. The *News* also indicated that most of the protesters "sang outside the . . . Airport terminal" for about "5 minutes," while "15 of their number entered the terminal without incident to present a resolution." But there was nothing to fear, the *News* implied, because the real focus of the story was on the law enforcement that had matters under control: "An air of tense expectancy prevailed at the airport as a crowd waited, some for several hours, for the Negroes to arrive, but the large number of city, county, and state law enforcement personnel gave the impression that the situation was well in hand. The tension seemed to disappear." The story was accompanied by a single photo of four Black ministers reading the resolution while three more look on—a total of seven Black protesters.[33]

The evening *Piedmont* provided a less neutral and more inflammatory narrative. "Airport Protest Is Held," read the small notice—on page 13—of the January 1 paper.[34] The next day's edition carried more extensive coverage on page 2, where the march was deemed "peaceful" and "march" was placed in quotation marks, suggesting somehow that the paper disagreed with the protesters' (and the rival *News*'s) description of the event. That assumption is borne out by the rest of the report, which was dominated not by the march but rather by remarks made by Ruby Hurley, NAACP field secretary in Atlanta. In a striking use of *pragmatographia,* the paper depicted Hurley as anti-White ("the only thing Whites have done for the Negro is to brainwash him"), anti-American ("America will not be able to convince a single person in Asia or Africa that it means right when 17 million colored people are 'enslaved'"), anti–South Carolina ("South Carolina has not produced a single statesman in all its history"), and anti-education ("Closing schools might be a good thing because then White folks and colored could grow up in equal ignorance"). The *Piedmont*'s small coverage of the airport march was limited to a reading of the resolutions the pastors presented at the airport. Two photos accompanied the story. In one, two Black ministers are shown at the airport, one giving the benediction. In the other photo, a line of Black marchers is depicted walking single file between law enforcement officers, supporting the story's contention that officials had warned marchers that "no disturbance was expected and none would be tolerated."[35] The description of the actual events in time, *chronographia,* follows the *pragmatographia,* which perhaps unwittingly apes the use of the figure in classical drama by describing events occurring offstage—Hurley's comments were used to imply that the real motives and thoughts and actions were nothing like what was being represented in the march. The result, of course, was a subtle suggestion that what the marchers were doing was not to be trusted: their appeals to God and to American values and to peaceful coexistence served simply as the pretty public face that covered a deeply cynical and antagonistic reality.

The rhetorical contest was engaged but not resolved. The airport, after bouncing between federal courts in a series of appeals and remands, was desegregated by court order on February 20, 1961. In the winter of 1960, however, the city of Greenville was a city on edge—everyone knew the airport stand-in was a beginning, not an end. No one knew what was next.

Students in the Library

Nearly two months after the airport stand-in, sixteen-year-old Ben Downs was sitting at his desk waiting for class to begin at Sterling High School. His friend Hattie Smith approached him and quietly told him that she thought he should join her in sitting in at the main branch of the Greenville Public Library. "I asked her," Downs said, "'You mean the White library?'" "Yes, I do," Smith replied. "OK," Downs said. Years later, when asked why he agreed to break the law so readily, Downs, a straight-A student, said, "Well, first of all, it was Hattie asking, and you don't say no to Hattie. And second, exclusion from that library and other good libraries always bugged me."[36] Downs's sentiments were shared by others in the Black community, especially students. By the middle of the twentieth century, American public libraries had become important sites of literacy and learning for many and an increasingly rhetorical space for some.[37] They had also become symbols of privilege, signifying access to and exclusion from education, the exchange of ideas, and civic engagement.[38] And from at least 1939, libraries had been contested.[39]

The main branch of the Greenville Library was at the time located on North Main Street. It was off-limits to the county's Black community, which had to make do with the McBee Avenue location. As several witnesses have since reported, the McBee location frequently had worn and tattered books that reached their hands only after White patrons had used them for years at the main branch and had a "spotty" collection a fraction of the size found in the main branch.[40] Acquiring books on interlibrary loan was sometimes impossible and, when possible, could take weeks.[41]

As stories of the sit-ins elsewhere reached Greenville like rumors of storm, student leader Hattie Smith and Rev. James S. Hall of Springfield Baptist Church went into action. Smith organized the students, and Hall helped coordinate adult support at his church and among the teachers at Sterling High School.

All knew they would eventually meet heavy resistance and that those who sat in were risking physical and verbal abuse of the worst kind—segregationists elsewhere had begun dumping hot coffee and chocolate on protesters' heads, spitting on them, yanking them from their seats, and frequently beating them. Sitting in required disciplined, passive, nonviolent resistance. And it frequently resulted in—and depended upon—arrests and jail.

The students tested both the segregated system and their own resolve on March 1. A loosely organized group of twenty to twenty-five students began walking to the main library. A few were picked up by the Reverend S. E. Kay of New Pleasant Grove Baptist Church when he responded to what he called a "hitchhiking signal" from them, and those in the car met those who had walked up North Main to the library. Accompanied by Kay, they entered the library at about 4:45 p.m., selected some reading materials, and sat quietly at tables reading. Kay reported that the head librarian, Charles Stowe, asked him to leave, as did F. Dean Rainey of the library board. When neither Kay nor the students left, the board of trustees decided to close the building for the night. At that point everyone, including the protesters, left the building. According to one of the students, they then met with Rev. Hall, who asked what had happened. When the students indicated they were told to leave or they would be arrested, they left.[42]

This first attempt to protest the library was clearly either poorly planned, improvised, or spontaneous. As Hall explained to the students, the whole point of a nonviolent sit-in was to get arrested and thereby call attention to the inequities of the library system and the city ordinances that supported them. Still the sit-in demonstrated that some Sterling High students not only had the resolve required to initiate a sit-in but also that the library was ill prepared to respond to a sit-in by orderly, neatly dressed, quiet, and studious teens. Moreover, the impression left by Jack Putnam, the one White eyewitness interviewed by the *News,* was of students using the library in entirely appropriate ways. When questioned by board member Rainey, Hattie Smith had indicated that the McBee branch did not have the books they needed, and they could not always wait for books to be sent to McBee. Kay testified that "nothing out of the way was said to any White person."[43] In short, though perhaps not as well planned as activists would have liked, the March 1 library sit-in nonetheless pushed back against Greenville's culture of segregation in important ways. By targeting the library and using it as it was intended—for reading and with seriousness of purpose—the sit-in undermined segregationist claims of Black intellectual and ethical inferiority and slovenly or disreputable lifestyles. It also resisted charges of disruption and outside agitation, for the students were quiet and all were Greenville residents.

The strategy of civil disobedience required arrests, however, and on March 16 seven students entered the library, sat down, and began to read. The "Greenville Seven" were, according to the *Greenville News,* Hattie Smith, eighteen; Doris Walker, seventeen; and Dorothy Franks, Blanche Baker, Benjamin Downs, Virginia Hurst, and Robert Anderson, all sixteen.[44] Librarian Charles Stowe once again told them that they "would have to use the McBee Ave. branch" for Blacks. The students refused. When police arrived they found the students "sitting quietly at three tables, or standing around," and later determined that they had not "said anything to anyone other" than Stowe, with no disturbance of the peace.[45] One officer said, "It was the nicest sort of thing. They were polite, quiet, and did as they were told."[46] When the police asked them to leave, the students indicated that they were in a public library, their parents paid taxes, and they had every right to be there. They were promptly arrested, booked, and released on bond after spending "about an hour" in jail, where the first song they sang was "America."[47]

The second library protest relied on and drew attention to its connections to the airport and first library protests but also shifted to new strategies, revealing different facets in the Greenville sit-ins' rhetorical trajectory. By singing for the short time in jail and making their first song "America," the students drew attention to their solidarity with the ministers at the airport. They also continued to undermine the segregationists' misanthropic vision of the Black community by dressing, sitting, standing, and otherwise behaving in ways that not only put the lie to the charges of social disruption, careless lifestyles, and sloth but also contributed to the impression of intellectual and ethical integrity, just as they had on March 1. But the students had also changed strategies. By voluntarily giving up their bodies for incarceration, they began to enact a complex somatic rhetoric of the law. Peter Goodrich explains that

> imprisonment implicitly renders the body docile and so amenable to instruction (*docere*) or inscription of law. The body is both the site and the conduit of submission of the soul to the "will of the law": arrest deprives the person of will so as to replace it, to bind it, to the meaning and form of law. While in one sense the superimposition of a collective intentionality upon the itinerant form of the person is unexceptional, there is also a more complex play of person and will, body and soul that deserves expansion. The law is staged through the body, and it is through corporeality, through the characteristics and qualities of the body and its movements, that the most profound substrates of law are to be read.[48]

By allowing themselves to be arrested, the students surrendered their bodies in the conventional sense and most certainly in the eyes of the public, Black as well as White. However they also precipitated a new action, allowing the law to be staged and challenged through their bodies—demanding, in a sense, that the legal question raised by their sit-in—is segregation lawful?—become, through the complex play of body and soul, should segregation be lawful? Put another way, the students' willingness to be imprisoned was the necessary first step of the legal battle to come: Was Greenville's inscription of segregation on the Black body forbidden by a higher law?

Later that year returning college students brought additional energy and determination to the youth movement, and on July 16 eight more students entered the library. The Greenville Eight were (again according to the *News,* with errors corrected in brackets), Benjamin Downs, seventeen; Elaine Leans [Means], Hattie Smith, Jeff [Jesse] Jackson, Joan Mattison, Doris Wright, Margaret [Margaree] Seawright, all eighteen; and Willie Wright, twenty. These students were also arrested, jailed for forty-five minutes, and released on bond. As in the March 16 sit-in, the students were "neatly dressed. The girls wore high heel shoes, and one of the boys wore a coat and hat. The others were clad in sport clothes."[49] By submitting their bodies to the law, they too joined the action precipitated by the March 16 sit-in, pushing the question of segregation's legality in the face of a higher law to the fore. The media coverage of this sit-in, the first to include a young Jesse Jackson, home from college for the summer,[50] included a photo of the students walking on Main Street and two more depicting them at the police station being booked. As received by the public, the July 16 sit-in was almost entirely somatic—few words were quoted, and the focus in the newspapers' accounts of the protest and arrest and in the photos that accompanied the stories was on their bodies—sitting, reading, walking, and surrendering themselves to the law.

Two days later the sit-ins moved to the lunch counters of Greenville's Woolworth, Green, Grant, and Kress variety stores, but the importance of the library sit-ins to Greenville's civil rights movement bears some mention. Libraries were sacred and symbolic public places, even more so because they represented, to the great-grandsons and great-granddaughters of slaves, a break from the last vestiges of the slave code's abhorrent literacy bans and an important step to full citizenship. On July 28 Robert Anderson and his father filed suit in federal district court, arguing that segregated public libraries violated the Fourteenth Amendment's equal protection guarantee. In response the library board voted to close all branches. On September 19, however, after weeks of anxious and agonized meetings of city officials—and perhaps seeing the future—they reopened as nonsegregated facilities, open to, in the words of Mayor Cass, "any citizen having a legitimate need for the libraries and their facilities."[51] Somehow they had won the struggle for the library. Like Black letters on a White page, the actions of these students—and all who followed their lead later that spring and summer—were read as invitations to reexamine not only the law but also the system of segregated public places the law supported.

Citizens at the Lunch Counters (and in the Churches and Skating Rinks)

Those involved in the Greenville sit-ins could not have known in the middle of July 1960 that a victory at the public library was two short months away and that the mere threat of federal action and more sit-ins would be enough to integrate the library by September. Their apparent willingness to subject themselves to arrest and imprisonment—to the authority of a law with which they disagreed—and their refusal to allow their dynamic and multimodal rhetoric to fall into any of the old segregationist traps frustrated the White establishment and encouraged the protesters. As Dorothy Franks and Ben Downs confirmed in a 2014 conversation, they felt "momentum building."[52]

The time felt right, but what was the next step? What strategic adjustments did the moment demand, and what direction should their rhetorical trajectory take? And what new challenges would they face?

As it turned out, they did not have (or take) long to think about these questions. On July 17, after attending the police court hearing for the Greenville Eight and feeling disappointed that the trial had been postponed to give time to have the jury trial requested by the city, activists staged sit-ins at Woolworth, Grant, and Green department store lunch counters. Violence soon followed. Charles Helms, a twenty-four-year-old White ministerial student from Atlanta, was "slapped around" and "roughed . . . up" outside the Grant store by "a group of White men," sit-in attorney Donald L. Sampson received bomb threats at his home, and the police received two anonymous calls, one of which predicted that there would be "bloodshed in Greenville before the night."[53]

Some have argued that nonviolent protest relies on a violent response for its effect, and certainly there are instances of this in the national sit-in movement. In Greenville, however, several key factors obviated against such a result. The national media were not in Greenville to cover the violence and local media were far less inclined to show White violence against nonviolent, nonresponsive Black activists. Additionally the chain department stores in Greenville had taken time to learn from their sister stores in cities where the sit-ins had hit the lunch counters first and simply closed the restaurant portion of the store and cleared everyone—Black and White—out before violence arose. Finally—and this is crucial—violence only advances nonviolent protests as long as they stay nonviolent.

The Greenville sit-ins did not. Less than a week after the sit-ins moved to the lunch counters of Main Street, the headlines blared, "Whites, Negroes in Street Battle."[54] The stories depicted a street fight that consumed an entire city block and involved at least thirty people, most of them youths. At least one source reported that the fights had broken out when "one in a group of White youths following the Negro demonstrators down Main St. leaped on one of the Negro youths from the back."[55] A lengthy fight ensued, ending only when local police and members of the South Carolina Law Enforcement Division (SLED) stepped in and arrested three local White students. A few days later, another fight broke out, this time in the parking lot of a "Kash and Karry" store. Police reported that the clash involved more than "200 teen-agers" and that "several shots" had been fired, but no one had been wounded.[56] A day later more fights broke out in downtown Greenville, and "half a dozen" Blacks and Whites were arrested. More shots were fired, and this time the media placed blame squarely on the Black community.[57] In an effort to "ease racial unrest," the Greenville City Council imposed a 9:00 p.m. curfew on all "persons 20 years old and younger."[58]

The sit-ins continued into August 1960 and so did the violence, which involved rocks, bottles, fists, and occasionally guns and knives. Most of the activists and segregationists were young. Parents, apparently, favored the continuing curfew, but the young people in the center of the things did not.[59] The curfew remained in place for most of what remained of that long, hot summer, and police continued to issue citations to young people involved in the fights, violating the curfew, and sitting in at lunch counters.[60] On August 9, 1960, fourteen young Black men and women staged a lunch counter sit-in at Greenville's S. H. Kress store and were arrested. Local news reported that they were the "first to be arrested" since the protests moved to the lunch counters. The ten who were sixteen or older were charged with trespass, jailed for several hours, and then released on bond.[61] They were convicted in Greenville's General Court of Session and appealed their case to the South Carolina Supreme Court.

While their case played out over the course of the next few years, Greenville's sit-in movement continued. During the 1960–61 academic year, Black students made concerted efforts to integrate the city. Several students sought to integrate all-White churches with a series of "pray-ins" at First Baptist and other downtown churches. The church struggle was more difficult in the wake of the violent summer and in a town known for its numerous Christian churches, both Black and White. And yet the very multitude of churches yielded part of the rationale for integration—churches, activists believed, were places in which a good deal of the city's business and politics were discussed, and exclusion from church meant exclusion from the conversation. Black students stood on the steps of the churches, talking with White congregants about their shared Christian faith and asking to pray together. Whites often ignored them, but occasionally a few engaged them in conversation. Eventually many White churches invited them in and allowed them to pray with willing White congregants.[62] In early 1961 other students sought to desegregate the local all-White skating rink operated by the city. Several students were arrested, and the city closed the rink rather than desegregate.[63]

As in the earlier phases of the movement, activists involved in the sit-ins of the late summer and fall of 1960 and the winter and early spring of 1961 once again shifted strategies. The most significant shift was one of place, as they moved their direct-action protests from fully public facilities and institutions to those that might be deemed quasi-public and others that were most certainly private. Churches, for example, enjoy tax-exempt status and also enjoy First Amendment freedom of religion protections. Lunch counters at variety stores were a different matter. While privately owned, they were not entirely segregated—Blacks could shop but not eat in them—and the city's segregation ordinances allowed private owners to exclude Blacks from the lunch counters if they wanted to.

The protesters—or at least some of them—also abandoned nonviolent modes of action and engaged those who physically accosted them. This move, while by no means unique in the larger civil rights movement, took away one aspect of their somatic rhetoric. Arrests for violent behavior could no longer represent a willing surrender of the body to the rule of law and the precipitation of an examination of the unjust law. In cases in which activists were charged with disturbing the peace, assault, or other violent acts, the law in question was not segregation. In cases of trespass, segregation was at issue and, as we will see, offered momentous opportunities for the kinds of change advocates most desired. In addition violent behavior played into the segregationist rhetoric of Black shiftlessness and ethical carelessness and allowed segregationists an opportunity to reclaim the moral high ground—the disturbance of good relations, after all they said, was triggered by Black integrationists attempting to change the long-accepted racial order and was perpetrated against law-abiding Christian business owners. Finally, out-of-town activists' participation in some of the sit-ins and some of the violence opened rhetorical space for segregationists' argument about the baleful influences of outside agitators on what had been, they said, a community of racial harmony.

Nonetheless by the summer of 1961, Greenville's White establishment began to worry about the effect the sit-ins and the growing racial disturbance would have on business in the city and state. They held conversations throughout the year and considered changes, in part due to their perception that the federal government would intervene and force the city and state to change public elements of its culture of segregation and in part due to the seemingly relentless pressure put upon communities by the sit-in protests. These changes coalesced in a speech given by prominent Greenville businessman Charles E. Daniel at the Hampton, South Carolina, Watermelon Festival on July 1, 1961. In "The Watermelon Speech," Daniel warned of the deleterious effects of a stubborn refusal to change and urged White South Carolinians to "forsake some of their old ways" and to take care of the segregation issue themselves before the federal government took even that choice away from the state.[64] His remarks were more timely than he knew, because, as he was delivering the speech, one of the legal cases involving Greenville's sit-in protesters was making its way through the South Carolina courts, heading to the federal government in the form of the U.S. Supreme Court.

Lawyers (and Judges) in the Courts

On March 22, 1960, just after the second library sit-in, the *Greenville News* ran an op-ed by syndicated columnist Ray Tucker. Titled "Negroes' Sitdowns Stir New Discord," Tucker's piece noted that neither President Eisenhower nor Vice President Nixon had "ever expressed an opinion on the question of Negroes' admission to privately owned facilities, where the management has a segregation policy and where local law does not require mixing of the races." He went on to note, correctly, that the "Supreme Court, in all its recent rulings, ha[d] not passed on this question," either.[65] He was correct—it had not. But it was about to.

The Greenville sit-in movement gave rise to many legal actions. As is often the case in American controversies, the rhetorical trajectory of a contested right, duty, privilege, concept, space, term, or condition of existence often includes or culminates in the legal forum. Part of this may be accounted for in the distinctly American tradition of judicial review of constitutional questions, part in our preference for rational, discerning judgment, and part, one might posit, in our very litigiousness. Whatever the explanation, the last phase of the Greenville sit-ins occurred in court.[66]

Several legal actions prompted resolution outside the court of the questions raised inside or were decided, settled, or dismissed as events unfolded. Richard Henry's case against the Greenville airport initially went against him in the federal district court when Judge George Bell Timmerman found that the "custom" of separate waiting rooms for Blacks and Whites at the airport did not amount to "state action" as required by the Fourteenth Amendment.[67] However, Henry appealed the case and eventually won in the Fourth Circuit Court of Appeals, where the court concluded that any action by the airport commission clearly constituted state action.[68] The library case, filed on behalf of the Greenville Seven,[69] was dismissed by federal district judge C. C. Wyche after city officials decided to close the library. Wyche ruled, as one reporter wrote, "that a nonexistent library cannot be integrated."[70] Still the case functioned as the student protesters wanted, for it pressured the city into reopening the library as an integrated facility. A third case, filed on behalf of the students who sought to integrate the city's all-White skating rink, was handled similarly by Judge

Wyche, who dismissed the case as moot when the city closed both of the city's skating rinks—one for Blacks and one for Whites—permanently.[71] Unlike the library case, however, the city did not move to reopen the skating rinks after the case was dismissed.[72]

However *Peterson v. City of Greenville,* the case that grew out of the August 9, 1960, lunch counter protests and arrests at Kress variety store, is a different matter altogether. *Peterson* raised the issue of whether the denial of service to Black patrons, by an essentially private business, on the basis of their race, met the "state action" requirement of the Fourteenth Amendment and accordingly violated the amendment's guarantee of equal protection of the laws.[73] The question was of considerable import before the passage of the Civil Rights Act of 1964 because it was an open question. "State action," required by part 1 of the amendment ("No state shall . . ."), was litigated in all of the cases above, and in *Henry* the federal district court and the Fourth Circuit Court of Appeals disagreed vehemently on whether actions by the Greenville Airport Commission rose to the level of "state" action. *Peterson* tested how far the Warren Court was willing to extend the theory of state action.

The facts of the case presented each party with a bit of argumentative purchase. On the one hand, the store manager had testified that he had asked the protesters to leave because to serve them would have been "contrary to local customs," strengthening the city's case that, if any discrimination took place, it was a private business decision and not a state action. On the other hand, the store manager also mentioned the Greenville city ordinance requiring separation of the races in restaurants.[74] At stake was an enormous slice of American urban and suburban life and a great deal of the culture of segregation.

Formally the sit-in protesters had been arrested and charged with trespass when they refused to leave the lunch counter when asked. At trial in the General Sessions Court of Greenville, special county judge James H. Price presiding, the defendants were convicted. They appealed to the South Carolina Supreme Court, which affirmed the lower court's ruling on November 10, 1961. Chief Justice Taylor wrote the opinion and was joined by Justices Oxner, Legge, Moss, and Lewis. Taylor dismissed the Fourteenth Amendment arguments by asserting that the defendants had been arrested and charged because they had remained in the restaurant after it had closed; all other patrons had left as requested, they had been asked to leave, and they had not. Taylor granted that the lower court record revealed that the restaurant was closed to follow its custom of serving Whites only but stressed that the state law of trespass under which the defendants were convicted made "no mention of segregation of the races" and therefore the decision to have them leave was a merely private one. He argued that "the Fourteenth Amendment erects no shield against merely private conduct, however discriminatory or wrongful, . . . and the operator of a privately owned business may accept some customers and reject others on purely personal grounds in the absence of a statute to the contrary."[75]

The protesters appealed, and the U.S. Supreme Court granted certiorari to "consider the substantial federal questions presented by the record."[76] The brief for petitioners was filed on September 19, 1962, and the brief for respondents on October 19, 1962. The Court heard oral arguments in the case on November 6–7, 1962.[77]

The protesters argued on Fourteenth and First Amendment grounds. On Fourteenth Amendment grounds, they argued that their exclusion from the lunch counter, along with their arrest and conviction, was required by a Greenville city ordinance that compelled segregation in eating facilities, and the exclusion, arrest, and conviction violated the Fourteenth Amendment's Equal Protection Clause.[78] In addition enforcement of segregation by the police and the courts of South Carolina, even in the absence of a law and the presence of custom, nevertheless still constituted state action.[79] Petitioners also asserted that the state's licensing and regulatory powers involved it deeply in the segregation policies of the stores and restaurants it licenses and regulates, again constituting state action, and that no essential property right of the Kress store was at issue.[80] The City of Greenville argued the proprietor of a privately owned restaurant has the right to serve only those whom he chooses and to refuse to serve those whom he desires not to serve for whatever reason he may determine and that there was no state action and consequently no denial of equal protection.[81]

The Court issued two opinions, a majority opinion authored by Chief Justice Earl Warren and a concurrence by Justice John Marshall Harlan II. Warren's majority opinion is stunning in its brevity and its dismissal of extraneous issues. After a review of the facts and a tight summary of the issues raised, he cut straight to the sole question the Court must answer: "Petitioners . . . assert that they have been deprived of the equal protection of the laws secured to them against state action by the Fourteenth Amendment."[82] Warren's tightly worded syllogistic argument has three parts: first, that the record demonstrates "beyond doubt that the Kress management's decision to exclude petitioners from the lunch counter was because they were Negroes";[83] second, that "the City of Greenville, an agency of the State, has provided by its ordinance that the decision as to whether a restaurant facility is to be operated on a desegregated basis is to be reserved to it," and the "Kress management, in deciding to exclude Negroes, did precisely what the city law required";[84] and third—and as a consequence—the convictions of the petitioners cannot stand, "even assuming, as respondent contends, that the manager would have acted as he did independently of the existence of the ordinance." The result, he held, was a "palpable violation of the Fourteenth Amendment [that] cannot be saved by attempting to separate the mental urges of the discriminators."[85] It is a hypothetical deductive argument: If there is state action that discriminates on the basis of race, that action violates the Fourteenth Amendment. There is state action that discriminates on the basis of race. Therefore, that action violates the Fourteenth Amendment.

Justice Harlan's concurrence is more nuanced. Though he reached the same conclusion in *Peterson* (there were five cases consolidated in *Peterson*, and Harlan did not reach the same conclusion as the Court in all five), he warned against assuming state action just because the ordinance existed. The central question, he believed, was whether the proprietor of a private business was acting of his or her own accord, based on private convictions and choices, or was coerced or influenced by the city ordinance. Because the manager's testimony at trial indicated both the restaurant's private choice and an acknowledgement of the city ordinance's demands, Harlan came down on the side of the protesters.

Peterson represents the last shift in the rhetorical trajectory of the Greenville sit-in movement. Far from the airport and the libraries, the lunch counters and the churches and the skating rinks, the movement's legal representatives took the protesters' bodies and their questions to the Supreme Court. In response to the question of whether Greenville's inscription of segregation on the Black body was forbidden by a higher law, the Court's answer was, yes, most certainly it was.

Conclusion

At the outset I suggested that Greenville's sit-in movement traced a dynamic, multifaceted rhetorical trajectory, one that arced across nearly three years and moved against a long-standing culture of segregated cohabitation. I have tried to highlight what I believe to be the most important facets—changing, multimodal persuasive appeals—and pivotal moments in the movement's course and to show how the movement adjusted to meet the shifting demands placed upon it not only by its circumstances and opponents but also by its own miscues and mistakes.

This study offers but one approach to protest movement rhetoric, but perhaps it offers some insight for the study of protest movements generally. For instance it seems to confirm Kendall Phillips's notion that, in our study of controversy, we might profitably focus on the intersection of moments of opportunity and specific sites of discourse instead of assuming a more or less static relationship between the public sphere and the controversial.[86] The Greenville sit-in movement progressed by seizing the opportunities presented by specific sites (and moments) of discourse and regressed by failing to seize (or perhaps recognize) other of those opportunities. In addition the study takes a decided posture in favor of case-based approaches to protest discourse and against predetermined or overly theory-laden approaches, preferring if possible to let the rhetorical strategies or discourses guide the study rather than force the study to try to corral the strategies and discourses.

Accordingly it is appropriate to end with a few words about the case at hand, the Greenville sit-in movement. Against all odds it succeeded about as well as a movement can, despite its mistakes. Martin Luther King Jr. later said about the sit-in movement generally that "as they were sitting in, they were really standing up for the best in the American dream . . . taking the whole nation back to those great wells of democracy."[87] It is fair to say that the Greenville sit-in movement, culminating as it did by breaching de jure segregation's last line of defense—"private" property—in *Peterson v. City of Greenville,* did more to advance democracy than the ministers, high school and college students, and even the lawyers involved ever imagined it could.

It did so despite succumbing to violence in the latter half of the summer of 1960. Whether justifiable or not, provoked (as it surely was) or initiated, the turn to violence did not help the movement. It gave segregationists rhetorical ammunition and gave those sitting on the fence pause. In the end it did not prevent the all-important legal case from moving forward, did not damage the case, and allowed the state's business leaders to make decisions favorable to the movement's goals. But it may have damaged the community and delayed its recovery from the turmoil. In 2000, decades after the events of 1960–63, Greenville erupted in another bitter battle, this time over recognition of the Martin Luther King holiday, and the state of South Carolina fought over the Confederate battle flag on its statehouse ground—placed there in April 1961—until it finally came down in the summer of 2015.

Still few of these difficulties can be attributed, directly or indirectly, to the Greenville sit-in movement or *Peterson v. City of Greenville.* The rhetorical legacy of the Greenville movement, like all protest movements, will continue to evolve as our understanding of it deepens and clarifies over time.

Notes

The author wishes to thank the librarians at the Greenville County Library, especially the staff of the Carolina Room and the library's generous director, Beverly James. The author also wishes to thank Jennie Hill for invaluable research assistance, Lesli Pace and Melody Lehn for helpful readings of this essay, Tierney O'Rourke and Rob Terrill for prompt and timely assistance in hours of need, and James Horner for the score of the motion picture *Glory.*

1. Black, "Gettysburg and Silence," 21–36. For further insight consider Terrill, "Rhetorical Criticism and Citizenship Education," 170–72. I am not aware of a study, other than this chapter, that considers the prismatic qualities of protest movement rhetoric.

2. Indeed it is known as Protagorean and Ciceronian *controversia* and has a rich literature. See, e.g., Mendelson, *Many Sides*; Sloane, *On the Contrary*; Conley, *Rhetoric in the European Tradition*, 37. For consideration of the larger issues found in rhetorics of

confrontation and controversy, see Scott and Smith, "Rhetoric of Confrontation," and Phillips, "Rhetoric of Controversy" (reconsidering the relationship between the public sphere and the controversial and suggesting a focus on the intersection of moments of opportunity and specific sites of discourse, issues upon which I touch at the end of this chapter).

3. The standard text on rhetorical history is still Turner, ed., *Doing Rhetorical History*. See, in particular, Zarefsky, "Four Senses of Rhetorical History."

4. Zarefsky, "Four Senses of Rhetorical History," 30. The earliest effort at studying rhetorical trajectories seems to have been Griffin, "When Dreams Collide." The current study takes added perspective from several others, including Kluver, "Rhetorical Trajectories of Tiananmen Square"; Ray, "Transcript of a Continuing Conversation"; and Dionisopoulos, et al., "Martin Luther King, the American Dream, and Vietnam."

5. *Brown v. Board of Education of Topeka*, 347 U.S. 483 (1954) (Brown I); and *Brown v. Board of Education of Topeka*, 349 U.S. 294 (1955) (Brown II).

6. "No Trouble Here Unless . . ."

7. Huff, *Greenville*, 257.

8. See Gordon, *Second Coming of the KKK*; Harcourt, *Ku Klux Kulture*; Hochschild, "Ku Klux Klambakes."

9. Huff, *Greenville*, 323–25, 357–58. See also O'Neill, "Memory, History, and the Desegregation of Greenville," 287.

10. On the lynchings between 1905 and 1933, see Huff, *Greenville*, 355–57. On the lynching of Willie Earle, see Gravely, "The Civil Right Not to Be Lynched"; and the William Gravely Oral History Collection on the Lynching of Willie Earle in the South Caroliniana Library, a division of the University of South Carolina University Libraries. It can be accessed online at http://digital.tcl.sc.edu/cdm/landingpage/collection/gravely. The international notoriety is largely due to Rebecca West, "Opera in Greenville." See also O'Rourke, "Racism's Lessons Learned in Upstate."

11. O'Neill, "Memory, History, and the Desegregation of Greenville," 288.

12. For differing accounts of White resistance generally, see, e.g., Lewis, *Massive Resistance: The White Response to the Civil Rights Movement*; and Webb, ed., *Massive Resistance: Southern Opposition to the Second Reconstruction*. For a sense of the rhetoric of this opposition, see Walker, "Legislating Virtue"; Mixon, "Rhetoric of States' Rights and White Supremacy." My account differs from these and seeks to attend to the interplay of regional and local themes.

13. Morton, *Crania Americana*; Cartwright, "Report on the Diseases and Physical Peculiarities of the Negro Race," originally published in the *New Orleans Medical and Surgical Journal* and *DeBow's Review* (both in 1851; the report was reprinted in many forms after). In his report Cartwright claimed to have discovered two diseases unique to African Americans: "Drapetomania," an illness that causes "Negroes to run away," and "Dysaethesia Aethiopica," which is the "natural offspring of negro liberty" and accounts for the African American tendencies "to be idle, to wallow in filth, and to indulge in improper food and drinks."

14. Landry, *The Cult of Equality*; Bilbo, *Take Your Choice*.

15. Brady, *Black Monday*. The book, originally delivered as a speech to the Greenwood, Mississippi, chapter of the Sons of the American Revolution, was widely read across the South.

16. "Decision of the Supreme Court in the School Cases." For interesting reassessments of what came to be called "The Southern Manifesto," see Day, *Southern Manifesto*; and Driver, "Supremacies and the Southern Manifesto." Most agree that the manifesto was originally drafted by South Carolina senator and Upstate resident Strom Thurmond.

17. *Greenville News,* June 7, 1960.

18. Workman, *Case for the South.* This work was followed quickly by James Jackson Kilpatrick's *The Southern Case for School Segregation* (n.p.: Crowell-Collier, 1962). Kilpatrick, then editor of the *Richmond News Leader,* was a frequent visitor to South Carolina, where he eventually retired.

19. Hill, "Reframing the Victim," 45–57.

20. Bob Jones Sr., *Is Segregation Scriptural?* (Greenville, SC: Bob Jones University, 1960). Original copies of this tract are extraordinarily and mysteriously rare these days. I am grateful to my friend and colleague Dr. Camille Lewis for her indefatigable work tracking one down and providing public access to it. See http://www.drslewis.org/camille/2013/03/15/is-segregation-scriptural-by-bob-jones-sr-1960/. See also Lewis, "A Is for Archive."

21. Jones, *Is Segregation Scriptural?* 8–10.

22. Ingram, ed., *Essays on Segregation.*

23. On the importance of the Cold War setting, see in particular Gilmore, *Defying Dixie* (demonstrating how radical reformers in the South made significant gains between 1919 and 1945, only to have them quashed by the second Red Scare and the Cold War). See also Egerton, *Speak Now Against the Day* (uncovering the stories of those who resisted the culture of segregation).

24. An earlier version of part of the following section of the essay was published in O'Rourke, "Circulation and Noncirculation."

25. As Jacqueline Dowd Hall has persuasively argued, neither the years 1954–68 nor even the broader frame of 1948–73 can contain the civil rights movement. See "Long Civil Rights Movement." On Greenville's civil rights struggle generally, see O'Neill, "Memory, History, and the Desegregation of Greenville"; and Hart, "Amend or Defend." For a more general view of South Carolina's civil rights history, see Lau, *Democracy Rising;* Hudson, *Entangled by White Supremacy;* and Moore and Burton, *Toward the Meeting of the Waters.*

26. *Henry v. Greenville Airport Commission,* 175 F. Supp. 343 (D.C. W.D.S.C. 1959); *Henry v. Greenville Airport Commission,* 279 F. 2d 751 (4th Cir, 1960); *Henry v. Greenville Airport Commission,* 284 F. 2d 631 (4th Cir, 1960).

27. For more details on the incident, see "Gloster Current to Robert Carter," in *First Class Citizenship,* ed. Long, 74–76. For Marshall's response to Robinson, see "Thurgood Marshall to Robinson," ibid., 79–80. For a general overview, with a sense of where the case fit in the larger national effort to desegregate airports, see Ortlepp, *Jim Crow Terminals,* esp. 36–89.

28. U.S. Const. art. I, §8, cl. 3.

29. Interview with Lottie Gibson, January 19, 2010.

30. "Negroes Conduct Orderly Segregation Protest Here." See also O'Rourke, "Greenville Airport Protest Started an Avalanche."

31. Goodrich, "Rhetoric and Somatics."

32. "Pilgrimage by Negroes Set Today."

33. "Negroes Conduct Orderly Segregation Protest."

34. "Airport Protest Is Held."

35. "Airport 'March' Peaceful."

36. Interview with Ben Downs, January 19, 2010.

37. By "rhetorical space" I mean not only sites or locations in which meaning—and motive, value, ritual, reason, and community—are performed and inscribed, but also the ways in which such locations hold and convey meanings of their own. See Middleton, et

al., *Participatory Critical Rhetoric*; Endres and Senda-Cook, "Location Matters"; Johnson, *Gender and Rhetorical Space*; Mountford, "On Gender and Rhetorical Space."

38. I am grateful to Janice Hamlet for this insight. Her unpublished draft manuscript, "Oh Mercy, There's Colored People All Over the Library" (in my possession), begins to explore some of the contours of the library as rhetorical space, and I have benefitted from her insight.

39. The year 1939 marks the date of the library sit-ins in Alexandria, Virginia. See Sullivan, "Lawyer Samuel Tucker"; "1939 Library Sit-In Anniversary." For a wider scope on public library integration in the civil rights movement, see Wiegand and Wiegand, *Desegregation of Public Libraries*; Knott, *Not Free, Not for All*; Battles, *History of Public Library Access*; Graham, *Right to Read*.

40. Judy Bainbridge reports that the main branch held 55,508 books and the McBee branch held only 11,644, "chosen, librarians said, to include those 'of most interest to Negro readers.'" Bainbridge, "Integrating Greenville's Library."

41. Interview with Hattie Smith Wright, July 10, 2010. Franks, Downs, and O'Rourke, "Communicating Civic Responsibility and Reconciliation."

42. Bainbridge, "Integrating Greenville's Library."

43. Walker, "Group of Young Negroes Enters Greenville Library."

44. Stokes, "7 Negroes Walk into Library Here." Bubbling just below the surface of the literature on the Greenville sit-in movement is a gentle jostling for history between the "Greenville Seven," high school students who sat in on March 16, 1960, and the "Greenville Eight," a mix of high school and college students who sat in on July 16, 1960. As I hope this chapter shows, both groups were important and perhaps even essential to the movement. The fact that the Reverend Jesse Jackson was a member of the Greenville Eight may account for its greater acclaim. I would point out that only two people, Hattie Smith and Ben Downs, were in both groups.

45. Ibid.

46. Ballenger, "City Library Calm during 'Sitdown.'"

47. Ibid.

48. Goodrich, "Rhetoric and Somatics."

49. Timms, "8 Negroes Sit-In at Library Here: Arrested and Jailed Briefly."

50. "The Greenville Civil Rights Movement," panel discussion at the Greenville County Library, Greenville, SC, 22 August 2013.

51. Eberhart, "Greenville Eight: The Sit-In That Integrated the Greenville (S.C.) Library." I cannot say that I agree with the title of this otherwise fine essay. As I think my chapter makes clear, all of the library sit-ins were important, and if forced to choose a "most important," I would go with 16 March.

52. Franks, Downs, and O'Rourke, "Communicating Civic Responsibility."

53. Ballenger, "Negroes Stage Sit-Ins at City Lunch Counters"; Timms, "3 Counter Sit-Ins Held in Greenville."

54. Thompson, "Whites, Negroes in Street Battle"; Ballenger, "Violence Flares on Main Street."

55. Thompson, "Whites, Negroes."

56. "White and Negro Teen-agers Clash."

57. "Gunfire Breaks Out as Races Clash in Greenville."

58. "9 pm Curfew Ordered to Ease Racial Unrest."

59. "Parents Unanimously Approve Curfew"; "Curfew Keeps City Quiet."

60. "New Sit-Down Staged Here."

61. Stokes, "14 Young Negroes Are Arrested after Sit-In."

62. Interview with Doris "Dee Dee" Wright and Leola Clement Robinson-Simpson, January 19, 2010, and interviews with Lottie Gibson, Ben Downs, and Leola Clement Robinson-Simpson, January 10, 2010. For images of the church campaign, see Robinson-Simpson, *Greenville County South Carolina*, 76, 86.

63. Zimmerman, *Negroes in Greenville*, 25–26.

64. Edgar, *South Carolina: A History*, 537–38.

65. Tucker, "Negroes' Sitdowns Stir New Discord."

66. On this movement from conflict to constitutional question, see Zarefsky and Gallagher, "From 'Conflict' to 'Constitutional Question.'"

67. *Henry v. Greenville Airport* Commission, 175 F. Supp. 343 (D.C. W.D.S.C 1959) at 351.

68. *Henry v. Greenville Airport Commission,* 279 F. 2d 751 (4th Cir, 1960); *Henry v. Greenville Airport Commission,* 284 F. 2d 631 (4th Cir, 1960). On remand Judge Timmerman expressed his exasperation with the appellate court by writing that "appellate court rulings, with which this Court heartily disagrees, are nevertheless binding and must be followed" and ruled in favor of Henry. *Henry v. Greenville Airport Commission,* 191 F. Supp. 146 (D.C. W.D.S.C 1961).

69. Walker, "Integration Local Library Is Sought."

70. Crocker, "Judge Dismisses Library Suit Here."

71. *Walker v. Shaw,* 209 F. Supp. 569 (1962).

72. A fourth case, *Whittenberg v. Greenville* (424 F.2d 195 [1970]), also arose out of the Greenville civil rights period. It involved integration of the Greenville schools but dates from beyond the period of the sit-in movement.

73. U.S. Const. amend. XIV, § 1.

74. Code of Greenville, 1953, as amended in 1958, § 31–8:

> (a) Separate eating utensils and separate dishes for the serving of food, all of which shall be distinctly marked by some appropriate color scheme or otherwise;
>
> (b) Separate tables, counters or booths;
>
> (c) A distance of at least thirty-five feet shall be maintained between the area where white and colored persons are served;
>
> (d) The area referred to in subsection (c) above shall not be vacant, but shall be occupied by the usual display counters and merchandise found in a business concern of a similar nature;
>
> (e) A separate facility shall be maintained and used for the cleaning of eating utensils and dishes furnished the two races.

75. *City of Greenville v. Peterson,* 239 S.C. 298, 122 S.E.2d 826 (1961) at 828.

76. *Peterson v. City of Greenville,* 373 U.S. 244 (1963) at 245.

77. The oral arguments are now available at *Peterson v. City of Greenville,* Oyez, https://www.oyez.org/cases/1962/71.

78. Brief of Petitioner at 14–21, *Peterson v. City of Greenville,* (No. 71) 373 U.S. 244 (1963).

79. Brief of Petitioner at 22–27, ibid.

80. Brief of Petitioner at 28–37, ibid.

81. Brief for Respondent at 3–15, ibid.

82. *Peterson v. City of Greenville* at 247.

83. Ibid.

84. *Peterson v. City of Greenville* at 247–48.

85. *Peterson v. City of Greenville* at 248. Christopher W. Schmidt reaches a somewhat different conclusion, arguing that the Supreme Court in *Peterson* reached the limit of what it was willing to do absent federal legislation. That legislation, as Schmidt shows, came in the form of the Civil Rights Act of 1964. See Schmidt, *Sit-Ins*, esp. 129–34.

86. Phillips, "Rhetoric of Controversy."

87. Martin Luther King Jr., "I've Been to the Mountaintop," text available online at the Martin Luther King Jr. Research and Education Center, Stanford University, http://king encyclopedia.stanford.edu/encyclopedia/documentsentry/ive_been_to_the_mountaintop/.

NOTHING NEW
FOR EASTER

Rhetoric, Collective Action, and the
Louisville Sit-In Movement

Stephen Schneider

On April 27, 1961, the *Louisville Defender,* Louisville's African American weekly newspaper, led with an article titled "What a Record? Louisville Leads Nation in Sit-In Arrests." The article described the 685 arrests that had occurred since February 20 of that year as part of a concerted campaign against segregation in public accommodations, a campaign that peaked with the "Nothing New for Easter" boycott of downtown businesses. However it was not only the high arrest total that made the campaign remarkable. Perhaps more surprising was that it occurred in Louisville, a city that was considered to be racially progressive in its laws and customs.[1]

This might also explain why Louisville's sit-in movement of 1959–61 is not as widely recognized as similar movements in Greensboro and Nashville. But despite its relative historical neglect, the "Nothing New for Easter" campaign and the sit-ins that led up to it provide important evidence both on the widespread adoption of the sit-in strategy within civil rights campaigns and the manner in which the sit-in as a form of direct action resonated among African Americans across the South. Sit-ins provided civil rights activists with a means of dramatizing their campaigns for integration and first-class citizenship, via the occupation of space that had hitherto been closed to them. As such sit-ins proved to be an important framing process—a means of interpreting injustice and coordinating direct action in response to that injustice.

In recognizing sit-ins as a framing practice, we might also recognize the way that sit-ins function rhetorically on both macro- and micro-mobilizational levels. Sit-ins not only dramatized injustice urgently and dynamically; they also fostered collective identity among participants and presented them with an immediate agency for collective action. Furthermore, insofar as they represent coordinated physical action, sit-ins speak both to the materiality of framing processes and to the manner in which collective action itself provides the foundation for the development of collective action frames among social movement participants.

Louisville and the "Nothing New for Easter" Campaign

Much like elsewhere in the United States, sit-ins in Louisville, Kentucky, focused on desegregating the city's public accommodations—particularly downtown lunch counters and department stores. While these sit-ins gathered momentum in 1959 and 1960, they nonetheless drew on prior efforts that extended back at least into the late 1940s. In fact, the sit-in as a strategy for desegregating public amenities in the River City had an even longer history: between October 1870 and May 1871, Louisville African Americans staged sit-ins on the city's streetcars and ultimately desegregated public transport.[2] This early campaign speaks not only to a long history of African American activism within the city of Louisville but also to the somewhat patchwork nature of segregation in Louisville—while public transport was integrated, segregation remained the custom in many other aspects of Louisville life. Nonetheless segregation was applied unevenly and to some degree unpredictably, suggesting to African Americans that it would require broad legislation on the part of city officials to eliminate racial discrimination from public facilities and accommodations.

By 1950 African Americans had already issued challenges to the segregation of public parks, golf courses, entertainment venues, and libraries. While early efforts met with important but limited success—Louisville hospitals began desegregating in 1949, as did the main branch of the Louisville Public Library, and the city's golf courses were opened to African Americans in 1952—segregation remained widespread in downtown department stores, theaters, restaurants, and lunch counters. The Louisville African American community called for legislation desegregating downtown businesses as early as 1954, with the city first considering such an ordinance in 1957.[3] Nonetheless city and state officials proved unwilling to further the cause of desegregation, citing questions of jurisdiction (uncertainty over whether desegregation was properly a city or a state issue) and the rights of private business to choose their clientele.

During the same period, Louisville's NAACP Youth Council and the Congress of Racial Equality attempted to pressure local business with sporadic sit-ins at lunch counters. Clarence Matthews, a reporter for the *Louisville Defender,* noted that African American journalists had already been testing segregation up to that point: "Some people forget this, but black reporters used to go out and test lunch counters, even before the students did in North Carolina. . . . I remember going in the old hotel, I think it was Fourth and Chestnut, and sitting down. And of course they refuse you, you go back and write a story about the refusal. . . . Black reporters used to do that all over."[4]

Matthews noted, however, that early efforts did not typically occasion the resistance leveled at later sit-in campaigns: "They just didn't serve me, that's all. They said, 'We don't serve Negroes here.' It wasn't any confrontation 'cause I wasn't being paid enough for that, to go to jail."[5] But whereas early test cases involved only individual reporters, sometimes accompanied by a photographer, the sit-ins that commenced in 1956 were a collective effort on the part of the city's civil rights leaders and students.

Lyman Johnson, a teacher at Louisville's Central High School and the plaintiff in the case that led to the desegregation of the University of Kentucky in 1949, led student sit-ins at drugstore lunch counters as early as 1956. The matter received further attention in 1958, when the visiting mayor of Kingston, Jamaica, was refused service at a Walgreens.[6] However these sit-ins did not coalesce into a wider movement until the Christmas of 1959 when African Americans decided to protest the opening of *Porgy and Bess* at the downtown Brown Theater. Despite the fact that the show featured an all–African American cast, African Americans were not permitted to attend the show.[7] The theater had, however, made tickets available via mail order, which allowed African American activists to organize protest actions outside the theater. Having purchased mail-order tickets, they attempted to take their seats for the show. As Raoul Cunningham recalls, "we already had our picket signs made. Once they turned the first group of us away, we immediately started picketing."[8]

The protests at the Brown Theater garnered wider attention than previous sit-ins and became a serious enough issue for the city to hold a public meeting about desegregation on January 7, 1960. While this led city aldermen to consider another integration bill in February, the ordinance was voted down, and action at the level of the city went nowhere.[9] In response African Americans initiated another round of sit-ins focused on downtown businesses generally and the Kaufman-Strauss department store specifically. "In contrast to comparable protests in communities across the South, however," Tracey K'Meyer notes, "these demonstrations did not spark mass daily demonstrations accompanied by nighttime rallies and arrests."[10] The protests did, however, coincide with the organization of the Non-partisan Voter Registration Committee—which ran widespread voter registration campaigns that summer—and local protests at venues such as the Algonquin Manor shopping center and Stewart's Dry Goods department store later in the year.

By 1961, however, sit-in protests were gaining momentum within the city. The success of sit-ins elsewhere in the region spurred local high school students and activists to once again engage in sit-ins at Kaufman-Strauss and Stewart's Dry Goods on February 9.[11] On February 20 five protestors were arrested; this, along with the increased media attention given to the latest round of protests, led to a sudden escalation of activity. The number of protestors increased to seventy-five on February 21, and sit-ins quickly expanded to more downtown restaurants, theaters, and department stores. Arrests increased as well, to a total of fifty-eight by February 24.[12] Aside from attracting the sorts of attention typically associated with civil rights sit-ins, these protests were also significant insofar as they gave birth to the "Nothing New for Easter" campaign.

"Nothing New for Easter" was intended to hit downtown businesses where it hurt in the lead-up to the 1961 Easter holidays. Protestors targeted both segregation and discriminatory hiring practices and encouraged African Americans to boycott businesses and cancel credit accounts with larger department stores. The campaign brought initial results relatively quickly, with Kaufman-Strauss and Stewart's opening negotiations with civil rights leaders by the end of February.[13] Mayor Bruce Hoblitzell likewise appointed a commission to examine the issue of desegregation and encourage dialogue between protestors and business owners.[14] But while the mayor had optimistically suggested that there might be a resolution to the issue by April 1, the failure to achieve concrete results by early March led civil rights protestors to hold a march downtown on March 10. Civil rights organizations including the National Association for the Advancement of Colored People (NAACP), the Congress of Racial Equality (CORE), the Student Nonviolent Coordinating Committee (SNCC), and the Southern Christian Leadership Conference (SCLC) also held events in support of the Louisville sit-ins, which reinforced the connection between local protests and the broader civil rights movement. In the same period, arrests continued to escalate to a total of 175 by March 15 and 685 by April 27—a number that Tracy K'Meyer notes were the highest in the nation to that point.[15]

Demonstrations were suspended during the 1961 Kentucky Derby (as much for fear of drunken reprisals against protestors as for respect for Louisville's signature cultural event) but began again soon after. Perhaps the most famous were the protests at the Fontaine Ferry amusement park, which began on June 19.[16] Protests against segregation of the park led local courts to issue an injunction against protests being held in front of the park, as well as a probation agreement with protestors that proved contingent upon them disavowing further protest activities. While the strong-arm tactics employed against the Fontaine Ferry protests attracted media and community attention, local activists also sought to organize the African American community in anticipation of fall elections. Their call for voters to vote for Republican candidates proved successful, and the elections saw many Democratic candidates suffer defeat in both mayoral and alderman races.

Continued activism by CORE and others in 1962 kept the pressure on the new city administration, and the overall efforts of civil rights activists eventually led the city on May 14, 1963, to pass an ordinance making it illegal to discriminate based on race in any public business.[17] Furthermore the Louisville sit-ins helped set the stage, along with similar protests in Lexington and Frankfort, for the eventual 1964 March on Frankfort to secure a statewide public accommodations law. While the legislation itself would not be passed until 1966, the march brought participation from national civil rights activists such as Rev. Dr. Martin Luther King Jr. and Jackie Robinson and culminated with a sit-in at the state capitol as civil rights protestors brought pressure to bear on state legislators.

Louisville's sit-in movement is noteworthy for several reasons. Not only does it speak to the widespread impact of the regional sit-in movement of 1960 and 1961, but it also highlights how sit-ins were already a recognized form of civil rights protest long before their widespread uptake during the classical period of the civil rights movement. Furthermore the "Nothing New for Easter" campaign allows us to understand better when and how sit-ins moved from being a civil rights strategy to an important movement in their own right. As I argue below, this shift also suggests a shift in how sit-ins function rhetorically, as they change from being primarily a form of public protest to also being a means of framing movement activity. Sit-ins, then, do not just provide protestors with a means of publicly communicating injustice; they also provide a means of organizing and fortifying collective action among movement participants.

Civil Rights Frames in the Louisville Sit-In Movement

It bears mentioning at the outset that the term *sit-in,* as it is encountered in descriptions of the protests in Louisville, designates a number of protest strategies: aside from sitting down at downtown lunch counters, Louisville civil rights activists also picketed theaters and bowling alleys, protested at drug stores and department stores, and boycotted segregated business in the lead-up to Easter 1961. As a result it might be asked how the sit-in movement emerged in Louisville and how that movement came to organize the civil rights struggles rhetorically within the River City in the late 1950s and early 1960s. Furthermore it might be asked how sit-ins, as a rhetorical locus for civil rights organizing, helped facilitate a shift from legal and political strategies to direct action in the fight against segregation in public accommodations.

The framing approach—an approach popular among sociologists looking at cultural and ideological aspects of social movement activity—may help understand the common identity that underpinned local forms of protest in the late 1950s. This approach examines how social movements establish various frames or "schemata of interpretation" that help movement participants understand

and respond to the world around them.[18] While the term *frame* is borrowed from the earlier work of Gregory Bateson and Erving Goffman, most movement scholars use the term to describe the collective action frames that social movements attempt to establish among participants and allies. Furthermore frames function as diagnostic, prognostic, and motivational structures: frames help individuals not only to attribute injustice and causality to social problems but also to develop and pursue potential strategies for social change.[19] As such, "collective action frames are action-oriented sets of beliefs and meanings that inspire and legitimate the activities and campaigns of a social movement organization (SMO)."[20]

Nevertheless Benford expresses doubt about the utility of simply identifying and describing movement frames: not only do descriptions often identify more frames than could be used in an explanatory sense, but they also overlook how frames are created and maintained by framing processes.[21] Put another way, framing approaches also recognize that movements are involved in important "signifying work."[22] Insofar as movements are involved in framing activities, "movement organizations and actors [are] actively engaged in the production and maintenance of meaning for constituents, antagonists, and bystanders or observers."[23] Frames emerge from and are transmitted by movement discourse, even as they determine in part what shape that discourse will take. As such they are as much rhetorical structures as they are cognitive ones, emerging from the interaction of movement participants and their interlocutors. Nor are these interactions limited to language: "frames can also be communicated through nonverbal devices, such as presentation of self, tactics, and organization forms."[24]

As rhetorical structures frames highlight important dimensions of social movement activity. First, they reveal that micro-mobilization (the recruitment and organization of movement participants) is as important a movement activity as macro-mobilization (the execution of protests and direct action campaigns.) Second, movements are constantly involved in the production of movement identity and culture. Third and finally, the rhetorical aspects of a movement's activities have a direct structuring effect on its collective identity and actions. Frames, then, might appear similar to Kenneth Burke's concept of terministic screens, which likewise serve to constrain rhetorically the manner in which individuals interpret and respond to the world around them.[25] However, where Burke's terministic screens might seem to function as ideological structures that determine worldview and rhetorical action, frames are more strategic. As such they describe not an ideological structure (which we might define as a complete system of values and beliefs) but rather a strategic arrangement of terms and concepts designed to garner support and structure response.[26]

An examination of the frames established by the Louisville sit-ins might help us understand how various protest forms came to be understood as extensions of a broader sit-in movement. In its most simple articulation, the collective action frame established by the sit-in movements of the late 1950s and early 1960s might be considered an extension of the master civil rights frame. This frame focused attention on African American demands for legal, political, and economic equality; defined segregation and Jim Crow as moral and legal injustices; and asserted the dignity and justice of African American efforts to secure their rights. Civil rights frames also informed and were in turn informed by the nonviolent direct-action campaigns that attended civil rights organizing across the South.

Sit-ins focused civil rights frames in a few key ways. First, sit-in frames were focused around the desegregation of public accommodations such as lunch counters, restaurants, theaters, and department stores. Sit-in frames also typically established the right of African Americans to request and expect service, with many sit-ins following a script that began with a request for service at a restaurant or lunch counter and became a refusal to leave without service if the initial request was denied. However, as the Louisville sit-in movement reveals, sit-ins also served as a rhetorical element within civil rights frames: they focused attention on the need for direct action in response to segregation, thereby helping to facilitate a shift from legal and political strategies for the mass campaigns associated with the classical phase of the civil rights movement.

The rights frame that Louisville activists drew upon had been formed much earlier than 1957, and civil rights activity was a constant feature of the city by that point. The frame that animated the sit-ins came from three key sets of events: local civil rights campaigns focused on integrating public accommodations in Louisville; larger national efforts to secure integration; and direct action campaigns such as those found in Montgomery and Greensboro. The existence of a strong NAACP chapter and an active African American newspaper, the *Louisville Defender,* meant there was also the infrastructure needed to tie these events together as a local movement frame.

In fact the *Defender* is a rich source for examining how civil rights frames developed in advance of and during Louisville's sit-in campaigns. While it should not be regarded as the only institution that contributed to frame development (nor should the frames presented in the *Defender* be considered the sole script for local civil rights activists), the *Defender* is an important source because it presented itself as a rhetorical agency for the expression of African American political aspirations. As an African American newspaper, the *Defender* overtly adhered to the Negro Press Creed, "that America can best lead the world away from racial and national antagonisms when it accords to every man regardless of race, color, or creed his human and legal rights."[27] In an editorial commemorating the 125th Negro Newspaper Anniversary Week, the *Defender* further articulated its mission as not just "[telling] of the failures and shortcomings of

Negroes" but also "[pointing] the way to overcoming these handicaps in order to reach the full stature of manhood."[28] The *Defender* thereby defined its role as the active articulation of a civil rights program that would serve and extend "the aspirations of Negros in Kentucky and America."[29]

By the early 1950s, the *Defender* had articulated its journalistic program to that of local activists. On the occasion of the paper's twentieth anniversary, its editors proclaimed that "because of their cooperation with the *Defender* and its ideas Negroes have made many openings where none existed before, they have been ready to grasp opportunities which if presented before could find no acceptable takers."[30] What the *Defender* brought to civil rights efforts in Louisville, then, was twofold. First, it provided an important vehicle for presenting local, regional, and national civil rights events, thereby aligning campaigns in Louisville with other campaigns across the country. Second, its editors provided clear interpretations of local civil rights issues as well as recommendations about how the African American community should respond. As a result they were involved rhetorically in developing local movement frames and aligning those frames with emerging national narratives about civil rights.

It also warrants mention that the *Defender* was staunchly committed to integration as the only means of achieving "first-class citizenship for all."[31] Local civil rights campaigns in the early 1950s likewise focused on the integration of public facilities. The Louisville NAACP chapter had already devoted considerable time to desegregating public libraries, schools, parks, and entertainment venues (primarily Memorial Auditorium and Iroquois Amphitheatre). In 1952 federal district court judge Roy Shelbourne ordered the integration of the city's golf courses in response to a lawsuit filed by African American dentist P. O. Sweeney. At the same time, African Americans were attempting to have segregated seating removed from Louisville's Parkway Field. By 1953, as the battle over park and amphitheater access continued alongside efforts to desegregate baseball games, the NAACP also turned its attention to the local interstate bus stations.

Buoyed by these efforts, *Defender* owner Frank Stanley wrote that "we have only scratched the surface":

> Segregation must be eradicated completely—especially in education, employment, and recreation. All public accommodations must be opened to us. There must be a Negro member of every policy-making body. Our immediate objective should be the Louisville Board of Education. Library integration should spread from the main library to all branches. Hotels, theaters, restaurants and stores should be opened to Negro patrons without restriction. In short, Kentucky should have a civil rights law that would prohibit any merchant or public accommodation from refusing service to a citizen

solely because of race. In addition, we need greater collaboration on every movement designed to make democracy a live, vibrant thing for everyone.[32]

We see in Stanley's remarks a full elaboration of the civil rights frame animating the *Defender*'s commentary in the early 1950s. William Gamson suggests that the basic architecture of collective action frames involves the coordination of three elements: injustice, identity, and agency.[33] Stanley hardly needed to identify the injustice associated with segregation, though he did situate it in opposition to a conception of democracy as a "live, vibrant thing for everyone." Furthermore this conception of democracy allowed Stanley to articulate African Americans' collective identity to a shared communal purpose and to efforts to define citizenship as a right not limited by race. Stanley also articulated the need for collective action, both when he exhorted readers to continue the fight against segregation and when he called specifically for "greater collaboration" in the interests of democracy. Perhaps most important, Stanley identified major sites of injustice—public accommodations, education, libraries, and representative bodies—and suggested that integration of one such site (in this case golf courses) naturally demanded integration of all of them.

It is worth noting that the collective action advocated by the *Defender* at this point was primarily focused on legal and legislative intervention—the securing of favorable rulings from judges or the election of local and national political candidates who supported civil rights legislation. For the most part, this was in keeping with the general strategies adopted by the NAACP, which remained Louisville's most prominent civil rights group until the late 1950s. Nonetheless, as the civil rights movement developed across the South and the nation, local groups came to focus increasingly on direct collective action—and the sit-in— as a complementary (or sometimes competing) strategy.

These campaigns received important rhetorical recognition when, on May 17, 1954, the U.S. Supreme Court ruled unanimously against the segregated public school in *Brown v. Board of Education* (347 US 483 1954). While the *Brown* decision had the partial effect of turning local NAACP attention toward school integration, it also provided an important master frame for local activists to align their efforts with; that the decision covered public education no doubt gave it even greater rhetorical resonance.[34] Reflecting on the importance of the case in May 1955, the *Defender*'s editors concluded that the case "[gave] legal sanction to moral obligation," thereby validating local efforts to combat segregation.[35] The master frame espoused in the *Brown v. Board* decision—one embodied in the language of the court decision itself—aligned with the local frames promulgated in the *Defender*. The focus was once again on integration as the only responsible means of achieving equality and on public institutions as the crucial battleground in that fight.

During the same period, the rights frame espoused by the *Defender* began to advocate direct action alongside support for the NAACP and other legal challenges to segregation. Commenting in 1955 on the still-segregated lunch counters at the city's train stations, the editors offered a pointed if oblique warning: "Better wake up, Louisville, to the inevitability of change—It is later than you think."[36] This warning followed what the paper perceived as unnecessary and unconscionable delays in the implementation of federal and Supreme Court decisions: as Frank Stanley put it, "the only way to integrate is to integrate."[37] It also anticipated the rise of massive resistance and the lack of federal response to increased violence against African Americans.[38] With the 1955 murders of George Lee, Lamar Smith, and Emmett Till, the *Defender* lost patience with a federal government that "has yet to intervene in a concrete way."[39] In the same issue, Stanley warned that "unless this reign of terror is abated in time, serious trouble is bound to come."[40]

Bus boycotts in Montgomery, Alabama (1955–56), and Tallahassee, Florida (1956–57), provided African Americans across the South with successful examples of direct-action campaigns. Frank Stanley remarked that "the Bus Boycott in Montgomery, Alabama stands out as an intelligent, organized method of making an effective fight against segregation" and that "their example is one worthy of emulation by others who would seek to better their lot."[41] A little more than a month later, Stanley reflected on the potential effectiveness of similar actions in Louisville.[42] By November the *Defender* concluded that "accomplished achievements were obtained by militant demands. Go-slowers and conservatives notwithstanding, other advancements will come only from more constant and militant demands for our just due."[43] It is significant that Stanley viewed direct action not just as a new means for responding to segregation but also as a means of responding to the failures of both government agencies and legal strategists to offer a serious challenge to racial prejudice.

We might suggest, then, that the militant demands championed by Stanley did not just establish direct action as another potential agency within the *Defender*'s rights frame; they also stood as evidence of an emergent collective identity among African Americans: "The hard facts are that Negroes no longer can be frightened on the issue of civil rights. In the case of buses some two dozen southern cities have desegregated them successfully. Moreover, in the cities of hard core resistance like Birmingham and Atlanta, Negroes are asserting their rights spelled out in recent court rulings. They can be depended upon to continue this movement irrespective of reprisals, trumped local evasion and temporary suspension of service."[44]

The *Defender*'s editorials speak to the dynamic nature of the rights frame they were espousing, which remained responsive not just to broader developments within the civil rights movement but also to the interrelation of injustice, identity, and agency. When legal challenges proved successful, they provided civil rights activists with new legal definitions of citizenship that in turn animated the conceptions of identity and agency that lay at the heart of local rights frames. That collective identity, however, increasingly looked beyond legal strategies to direct action as an agency for achieving their demands.

The increased attention toward direct action coincided with a renewed attention on public accommodations. Focus had already turned to public accommodations by 1956, when the January 19 issue of the *Defender* ran the front-page headline "Lunchrooms Still Segregated Here" in reference to waiting rooms and restaurants at city train stations.[45] Clarence Matthews and Frank Stanley again returned to the topic in November 1956, focusing on segregation in restaurants, theaters, bus terminals, and hotels.[46] However the issue received sustained attention in December 1958, following the refusal of a Walgreens drugstore to serve the visiting mayor of Kingston, Jamaica. The *Defender*'s editors immediately decried the event as an insult and called for a public accommodation ordinance to address the problem.[47] In the same issue, journalist Nat Tillman began what would become an eighteen-story series on the segregation of public accommodations in Louisville. The series—along with nineteen other editorials and articles devoted to segregation in Louisville's public accommodations—not only emphasized segregation as a widespread issue across downtown Louisville but also kept the subject on the *Defender*'s front page until April 1959. Throughout those months the injustice posed by downtown segregation once again became a "hot cognition," a site of moral indignation that required immediate redress.[48]

It was this elaborated rights frame—one in which segregation in public accommodations became a hot cognition to be remedied by legal and protest actions—that animated sit-ins throughout 1959, first at Taylor Drug Stores and then at the American Legion and the Brown Theater.[49] It also informed Tillman's argument that "the examples set by the Committee of Racial Equality [*sic*] in its effort to break down racial discrimination have plenty of merits and could very well be utilized by other groups opposing segregatory practices."[50] Tillman drew attention to CORE sit-ins occurring in St. Louis and closer to home in Lexington and argued for similar sustained activities in Louisville. The Christmas pickets of the Brown Theater further assured that this frame would continue to have resonance as Louisville's emerging sit-in movement headed into 1960. Reflecting on the failure of city and state public accommodations ordinances, the *Defender*'s editors concluded that "wisdom, therefore, dictates a consolidation of effort toward winning the battle first in Louisville, where there is some evidence of desegregated public accommodations."[51]

Remarks by Tillman, Stanley, and the *Defender*'s editors prove significant insofar as they suggested the need for a shift in strategy—from legal action to direct action—and the adoption of CORE protest strategies alongside those of the NAACP. However to suggest that direct action became an increasingly central aspect of civil rights frames within Louisville is not to suggest that activists gave up on legal and political strategies. Much of the *Defender*'s attention on the issue then turned to the efforts of Alderman W. W. Beckett to introduce a city public accommodations ordinance, efforts that continued without success for much of the year. (Beckett twice brought ordinances before the city council—once in February and once in March—only to have them voted down on both occasions in favor of voluntary desegregation.) Nonetheless the outrage that followed the defeat of Beckett's efforts was expressed within the context not just of intransigent city politics but also of the emerging sit-in movement. The *Defender* first noted the sit-in movement on March 3, devoting front-page space to the spread of sit-ins as a "vital force to be reckoned with."[52] A week later, an editorial titled "It Can Happen Here" linked the failure of city desegregation efforts directly to the potential for sit-in protests in the River City: "For the moment Louisville has been spared of renewed protest demonstrations. They will not be forever absent, however, if Mayor Hoblitzell, the Board of Aldermen and segregating businesses continue to underestimate the extent of Negro dissatisfaction with the 'Status Quo.'"[53]

The *Defender*'s editors recognized that the political opportunity structure surrounding the issue of public accommodations in Louisville had shifted in important ways. The city's civil rights activists had been challenging segregation of public facilities for more than a decade, and landmark federal legal decisions had served only to strengthen their resolve. Furthermore civil rights campaigns in Montgomery, Tallahassee, and later Greensboro provided activists with new protest strategies and with evidence of those strategies' efficacy. The rhetorical figure of the sit-in, alongside the material practice of sitting in, came to organize civil rights rhetoric in the River City and led activists to read events in Louisville in the context of emerging direct-action campaigns across the South. It is this shift in political context that led both to the widespread adoption of sit-in strategies by Louisville's civil rights campaigners and to the use of sit-ins across the region as a rhetorical lens for discussing local civil rights struggles.

The Sit-In as a Framing Practice

As Louisville's sit-in movement gathered momentum in the early months of 1960, CORE activist Rev. James Lawson visited Louisville to help local NAACP members coordinate their civil rights activities. Lawson advocated sit-ins as a logical means of pursuing nonviolent resistance to segregation and racial prejudice and specifically identified four key aspects to such nonviolent direct action. First, such action drew attention to segregation as an "immoral, unjust, and sinful" institution. Second, a nonviolent action brought about "Christian change" in a faster manner than legal action. Third, a nonviolent action allowed African Americans to discover "new concepts of themselves in this new spirit of disciplined unification." And fourth, nonviolence created an "atmosphere in which social change can take place."[54] In offering these four points, Lawson not only reflected on the theories of nonviolent resistance then developing among CORE, SNCC, and SCLC members; he also sought to align local civil rights frames in the River City with those developed elsewhere across the South. These new civil rights frames—which were immediately linked to the emerging regional sit-in movement—would, in turn, animate sit-in protests in Louisville throughout the early 1960s.

Lawson's remarks are also important as a description of how the sit-in strategy was not only animated by civil rights frames but also an increasingly important element within those frames. Furthermore his four points suggest that he understood sit-ins not just as a protest strategy but rather as material rhetorical structures that enabled activists to dramatize and disseminate civil rights frames. As suggested above, the sit-in frame espoused by Louisville's civil rights activists not only drew on earlier rights frames but also served to organize a range of activities—from the Brown Theater pickets to lunch counter sit-ins, to the "Nothing New for Easter" boycotts. Frank Stanley even referred to the need for a "vote-in" in the 1961 city elections, suggesting that even more conventional political organization could and should now be understood within the context of local direct-action efforts. Sit-ins, then, were not simply the manifestation of already extant rights frames; rather they were an important rhetorical agency for developing and maintaining those frames.

Most immediately sit-ins dramatized the injustice of segregation as an urgent issue in need of immediate remedy. In an editorial republished in the *Defender* in March 1960, the *Philadelphia Tribune* argued that "the one thing already accomplished by the demonstration of Negro students in the South is to disprove the assertions of Southern politicians that Negroes are satisfied with segregation."[55] Reflecting on local conditions, Stanley echoed this sentiment when he suggested that "considerable Louisville Negro souls are tired enough right now to rise up in righteous indignation."[56] Sit-ins became the natural outpouring of African American demands for justice, which increasingly highlighted the lack of progress made via political or legal avenues. Indeed by 1961 the *Defender* claimed that sit-ins "were born in the persistent denial of Public Accommodations privileges and the total lack of official leadership given to this issue."[57] Sit-ins, then, established the *kairos* of the public accommodations battle materially, in much the manner that King argued in his "Letter from Birmingham Jail" that African Americans could no longer wait for White approval or assistance on the issue of civil rights. "The only way to obtain your rights," concluded the *Defender*'s editors, "is to nonviolently clamor for them."[58]

Sit-ins did not always decry the injustice of segregation in strident terms; humor and irony proved to be just as effective in highlighting the arbitrary and ultimately indefensible segregation policies of local businesses. The *Defender* noted that, during negotiations over the Algonquin shopping center pickets and attempts to desegregate the center's bowling facilities, "two fair skinned Negroes . . . were completing games on one of the lanes' 72 alleys."[59] Mervin Aubespin discussed a similar set of events that occurred at the Blue Boar restaurant during downtown sit-ins in 1960 and 1961:

> A guy named Johnson owned the Blue Boar chain, and there were about three restaurants local [*sic*]. But there was one at Fourth and Chestnut Street. He was also president of the Restaurant Association, and a member of the Board of Education. And it was a fast place, it was a cafeteria like place that was quite popular at noon. We focused on it, because it was the type of place that all economic levels felt comfortable in, but blacks were not allowed in there. And one day, in order to show how ironic it was, and he was a hard egg to crack, we sat my mother, and a number of members of the African American community, who were extremely fair and you couldn't tell the difference. People like Marjorie Miles, who was as white as this cup with straight hair and others, but then you know, we've just got that whole rainbow thing. And there were a number of them, who were that fair, that you couldn't tell. And we had them to go, they went, and not in a group, two at a time, three here, just like they were going in. And they were seated all over the place. And then their husbands arrived to meet them. And of course, they stopped them at the door. And it made the point so beautifully: it was interesting that I never saw anything in *The Courier-Journal* about it.[60]

The Blue Boar protests highlighted the uneven application and enforcement of segregation customs in Louisville. Aubespin's reflections on the humor involved in the process also demonstrate how the protest challenged not only the arbitrary nature of desegregation but also the faulty logic underlying the use of skin color as a dividing line.

However, just as important, sit-ins did not simply articulate a goal or demand equal service; rather they established African American rights via an occupation of public space. The very nature of their demands—for a sandwich or a cup of coffee, without having to move—made any attempt at "reasonable" resistance all but impossible. By physically enacting their demands, sit-in participants also highlighted the inadequacy of calls for voluntary action on the part of business owners, who in turn claimed to be waiting for other business to make the first move. Insofar as they dramatized injustice and provoked visible responses from business owners, sit-ins proved capable of capturing the public imagination in a way that newspaper articles and legal strategies had not.[61]

The sit-in became a performative rhetorical strategy—one that dramatized the claims of civil rights activists by enacting materially the behaviors that they hoped to have protected by law. As one editorial on the May 1960 Kaufman-Strauss pickets put it: "We do not know how Vice President, Roy Gardner will determine when its Tea Room integration will be right. But it has been 'right' all along—the principle of fair play and common service to all customers alike, that is. There is no justifiable argument against the rightness of integration. It is one of those things almost everyone agrees should be done. But few do anything to achieve it."[62]

Sit-ins, then, were an attempt to achieve integration, and to do so in the faster manner identified by Lawson. However they were also an attempt to intensify the claim that integration was an indisputable moral right by enacting integration counter to legal or social custom. Sit-ins thereby begged the question—why can't everyone be served?—by dramatizing both the question and its only reasonable answer in the most urgent of terms.

The demands of local picketers were no doubt strengthened by the other local and regional efforts being made to combat segregation. Stories following the regional sit-in movement appeared on the front pages of the *Defender* alongside articles devoted to Alderman Beckett's battles with the city board.[63] Sit-ins became a means of demonstrating the shared identity of civil rights campaigns—whether focused on legal or direct action, whether local or regional in scope—and further framing local civil rights campaigns regarding shared principles. A front-page editorial published on January 7, 1960, indicates the framing potential to be found in the December 1959 pickets of the Brown Theater: "The current picketing is actually not against the Brown Theatre alone, nor is it a clamoring just to see Porgy and Bess. . . . However, the principle remains: Why cannot Negroes go to movie houses unsegregatedly in Louisville? Would it not seem that races that can swim, play, study, read, work and in some instances worship and eat side by side certainly could sit together at a movie?"[64]

Concluding that protests were necessary for the face of lingering prejudice and neglect by city officials, the editorial argued that the only actions open to "all people of good conscience" were both to join the picket line and apply pressure to city officials and theater owners.[65]

However, just as important, sit-ins provided an immediate representation of local rights frames. Commenting in March 1961 on the momentum and the achievements of the sit-in movement, Frank Stanley noted that "the manner in which Louisville Negroes are making their clamorous demands felt—the coordination of effort and the depth of solidarity all are wonderful sights to behold. The movement in itself without any real test of strength has won many white supporters."[66] What Stanley's remarks make clear is that sit-ins themselves structured and fostered collective identity, suggesting that the coordination of effort emerged from the dynamic structure of sit-in protests. However coordination—the coordination of sitting down together, picketing together, and maintaining the composure needed for nonviolent action—is just as important as the sense of shared purpose that Louisville's civil rights activists had. By engaging in the coordinated activity, activists created what Gladys Ritchie has called a "rhetoric of human action."[67] For Ritchie such a rhetoric inheres not only in the manner in which the sit-in participant's body becomes a vehicle for displaying and protesting an injustice but also in the way that participants act together: "Greensboro, 1960. Surrounded by a large crowd of white high school toughs dressed in black leather jackets and carrying Confederate flags, a group of integrated students sat-in at the Kress lunch counter. The students were very well dressed, many in suits and ties and several carried Bibles. While the young whites taunted, snarled and jeered, the students remained silent, poised, determined."[68]

What becomes important in this description is the shared activity of wearing suits, carrying Bibles, remaining silent in the same pose. These activities become an instance of what historian William McNeill has called "keeping together in time," the coordinated physical aspects of dance and drill that create in participants a feeling of solidarity and membership within a group.[69] If we acknowledge sit-ins not simply as a protest strategy but also as an instance of a coordinated physical action, then we might see similar dynamics at work within those protests as well.

If we understand sit-ins as a rhetorical practice, then Stanley's comments demonstrate the manner in which sit-ins and collective action made civil rights frames both visible and rhetorically effective. The collective action itself becomes a crucial means of cultivating collective action frames and not simply the desired output of other framing efforts. Furthermore Stanley's comments describe how the sit-in as a rhetorical practice also allowed the amplification of civil rights frames for White sympathizers. While collective action as a framing practice no doubt exists in a somewhat reciprocal relationship with extant and emerging civil rights frames, its foundational importance as a framing practice demonstrates how sit-ins worked rhetorically on both macro- and micro-mobilizational levels.

With the emergence of the sit-in movement in Greensboro and other southern cities, the *Defender* had further evidence of the efficacy of sit-in protests.[70] Efficacy, however, was framed not simply in terms of sit-ins' disruptive force, nor their dramatization of the just demand for access to public space, but rather in terms of economic impact. "Next to his ballot," stated a March 1960 editorial, "the Negro's buying power is his most potent weapon."[71] Dean Gordon Hancock, writing only two weeks later, noted that the sit-in movement was by now "the top controversy in the United States."[72] However the importance of the sit-ins for Hancock was, once again, economic: "The current sit-downs are attempts to emphasize the possibilities in making the dollar do double duty, by using it as a weapon against segregation and as a protest against restricted economic opportunities."[73] The collective identity found in sit-in protests was aligned with a collective economic identity that might have been less easily recognized. Nonetheless as boycotts continued and stores elected to shut rather than integrate their restaurants, this collective economic force became more and more apparent. As one editorial put it: "The sit-in and the economic boycott are the surest signs that a new era in race relations in the South is underway. They are signs that there is a deep convention [*sic*] among Negroes that they can wait no longer in starting programs to achieve what they consider to be their rights."[74]

The arguments found within the *Defender* also suggest that local sit-ins increasingly came to invoke the regional sit-in movement and thereby functioned rhetorically as a reference to struggles against segregation across the South. Furthermore the *Defender* aligned the rights frames of local protestors with similar frames held by individuals sympathetic to the cause of civil rights. An editorial reprinted by the *Defender* in March 1960 argued that, in the face of the escalating sit-in movement, "surely [President Eisenhower] does not consider it lawful for Negro American citizens to be thrown in jail by the hundreds and showered by tear gas bombs simply because they seek to have the same privileges enjoyed by other Americans."[75] Chastisement of the president's inaction served not only to highlight the injustice of federal inaction but also to rally those readers who agreed with the editorial's depiction of the moral character of the sit-in movement. The *Defender*'s editors likewise encouraged local African Americans to align their actions with the sit-ins underway at the Brown Theater, Kaufman-Strauss, and Taylor. This attempt at frame alignment likewise came via censure of those not boycotting protested businesses: "The very least side-line-sitting Negroes can do is to have enough self-respect to stay away from businesses that segregate."[76] Sit-ins served as a means of elaborating and disseminating local civil rights frames via collective action itself and as a means of inviting support and participating from like-minded citizens for whom the sit-ins resonated.

Sit-ins thus proved to be important forms of collective action on both macro- and micro-mobilizational levels. That they also functioned rhetorically as dynamic framing processes can be seen in the formation of the Student Nonviolent Coordinating Committee, which itself emerged in part as an expression of the collective identity that had formed between sit-in participants across the South. The centrality of the sit-in strategy even led one Associated Negro Press article to refer to the movement as "sit-downism."[77] This process of identity formation also functioned as an agency for directly pursuing social change. Frank Stanley directly linked both processes when he remarked that "all social progress—all crusades have had . . . radicals, whom I prefer to call people so endowed with a sense of freedom that they will speak up and out at all times against human injustice. These bold expressionists have now been buttressed by those who stand-in, sit-in and kneel-in."[78]

Conclusion

The Louisville, Kentucky, sit-in movement played an important role in the development of the city's civil rights movement within the River City. The protests that culminated in the "Nothing New for Easter" campaign represented a shift among local activists from campaigns centered primarily on legal and political assaults on segregation to those based on nonviolent direct action. These campaigns not only had the effect of calling into question the efforts of local and federal officials but also highlighted the existence of widespread racial injustice in a city that had been regarded as one of the more racially progressive in the South. As depicted in the *Defender,* local sit-ins gave lie to the notion that African Americans were content with their lot and dramatized the injustice they faced in restaurants, parks, sports facilities, and bus stations. Furthermore segregation was not simply a sectional problem: by aligning their efforts with those of civil rights activists across the South, Louisville's civil rights movement drew attention to racism as a problem faced by African Americans everywhere.

The "Nothing New for Easter" campaign provides a rich archive for the study of the rhetorical dimensions of sit-in campaigns. Sit-ins proved to be important rhetorical actions not just on a macro-mobilizational level (where they served to highlight and challenge directly the injustice of segregation) but also on the micro-mobilizational level (where they served to coordinate civil rights activists and foster collective identity among African Americans and sympathetic Whites). But perhaps most significant is the manner in which sit-ins, as a form of coordinated activity, made coordinated collective action itself the rhetorical foundation for the creation and elaboration of civil rights frames. Far from being the simple product of prior framing activities (though the Louisville sit-ins did emerge in part from the rights frames already articulated in the *Defender* and the African American community), sit-ins became a material framing practice in their own right and made possible the broader dissemination of rights frames.

The Louisville sit-in movement also highlights the way that the sit-in functioned as a rhetorical structure to organize a range of protest activities in a coherent set of campaigns. The rhetorical role of the *Louisville Defender* in fomenting Louisville's sit-in movement and also in interpreting and amplifying that movement's demands further emphasizes the manner in which sit-ins worked rhetorically to extend and transform earlier civil rights frames. The arguments presented by the *Defender*'s editorial staff also make clear that the sit-in frames developed by Louisville's civil rights movement extended beyond the simple act of sitting in and provided a means of interpreting the city's civil rights history. These frames not only served as an extension of earlier frames focused on legal and political strategies but also as a pointed response to those frames. Locally sit-ins spoke to the failure of city administrations and government officials alike to achieve meaningful civil rights reforms and to the need for African Americans to assert the rights they hoped to have recognized under the law.

While it remains important to locate civil rights sit-ins within the broader historical context of the civil rights movement, and also to locate the sit-in frames constructed by the Louisville sit-in movement within the broader civil rights frames operative within Louisville's African American community, the study of these sit-ins as framing practices provides a means of better understanding how collective action operates within social movements as a form of rhetorical action. Sit-ins were able to dramatize the injustice of segregation via the occupation of public spaces to which all citizens should have access. While the coordinated collective action found in such protest strategies as marches, singing, pickets, and sit-ins always takes place within the broader context of a specific social movement, such actions remain an important means of animating, maintaining, and furthering that movement's identity and influence. Collective action not only offers a means of communicating a movement's goals and demands; it also provides a structure for creating a collective identity and deploying that identity as an agency for social change.

Notes

1. "What a Record?" See also K'Meyer, *Civil Rights in the Gateway to the South,* 91.
2. Norris, "Early Instance of Nonviolence."
3. K'Meyer, *Civil Rights in the Gateway to the South,* 80.
4. Fosl and K'Meyer, *Freedom on the Border,* 88.
5. Ibid., 89.
6. K'Meyer, *Civil Rights in the Gateway to the South,* 81.
7. Fosl and K'Meyer, *Freedom on the Border,* 92.
8. Ibid., 92.
9. K'Meyer, *Civil Rights in the Gateway to the South,* 83.
10. Ibid., 85.
11. Ibid., 87.
12. Ibid., 88.
13. Ibid., 89.
14. Ibid., 91–92.
15. Ibid., 90–91.
16. Ibid., 97.

17. Ibid., 77.

18. Snow et al., "Frame Alignment Processes," 464.

19. Benford and Snow, "Framing Processes and Social Movements," 615.

20. Ibid., 614.

21. Benford, "Insider's Critique of the Social Movement Framing Perspective."

22. Snow and Benford, "Master Frames and Cycles of Protest," 136.

23. Ibid.

24. Noakes and Johnston, "Frames of Protest," 8–9.

25. Burke, *Language as Symbolic Action,* 44–63.

26. Zald, "Culture, Ideology, and Strategic Framing."

27. "Negro Press Creed."

28. "Negro Press Is You."

29. Ibid.

30. "Our Anniversary."

31. Stanley, "Being Frank," August 18,1951.

32. Ibid., April 2, 1952.

33. Gamson, "Constructing Social Protest," 90.

34. Bell, *Silent Covenants,* 35.

35. "Notable Anniversary."

36. "How Not to Attract."

37. Stanley, "Being Frank," January 6, 1955.

38. "Federal Intervention Necessary."

39. "Mississippi Injustice."

40. Stanley, "Being Frank," September 15, 1955.

41. Ibid., February 9, 1956.

42. Ibid., March 15, 1956.

43. "Militancy Is the Watchword."

44. "Groans from Dying Practices."

45. "Lunchroom Counters Still Segregated Here."

46. "Louisville Public Places Present Dismal Picture of Discrimination"; Stanley, "Being Frank," November 29, 1956, December 6, 1956.

47. "Ordinance Needed to End 'Accommodations' Bias."

48. William Gamson, "Constructing Social Protest," 90.

49. "Public Accommodations Bias Protest Begins"; "Wave of Protest Gets Legion Action"; "NAACP Pickets Brown Theater."

50. Stanley, "Being Frank," August 20, 1959.

51. "Better Strategy."

52. "Student 'Sit-Ins' Emerge as a Vital Force."

53. "It Can Happen Here."

54. "Sit-In Leader Advises Appeal to Moral Issues."

55. "Sit-Downs Prove Negroes Not Satisfied."

56. Stanley, "Being Frank," April 21, 1960.

57. "Crisis of Conscience."

58. Ibid.

59. "Bowling Segregation Is Cause of Disagreement."

60. Aubespin, Brinson interview, 24–25.

61. "Brown Theater Protest Points Up Bias Problem."

62. "Can't Eat—Don't Buy."

63. "Aldermen 'Kill' Human Relations Bill"; "Citizens Rally to Hear Core Leader"; "Students Win Sit-In Victory in N.C. Court"; "Sit-In Leader Lawson at NAACP Meet Here."

64. "Editorial."

65. Ibid.

66. Stanley, "Being Frank," March 9, 1961.

67. Ritchie, "Sit-In," 22.

68. Ibid.

69. McNeill, *Keeping Together in Time.*

70. "Student 'Sit-ins' Emerge as a Vital Force."

71. "It Can Happen Here."

72. "Student 'Sit-Ins' Is Top Controversy in United States."

73. Ibid.

74. "Sit-Ins, a Weapon of Choice?"

75. "Sit Downs Prove Negroes Not Satisfied."

76. "Sit-Ins, a Weapon of Choice?"

77. "Students Form Non-violence Coordination Group."

78. Stanley, "Being Frank," September 22, 1960.

THE CHARLOTTE, NORTH CAROLINA, AND ROCK HILL, SOUTH CAROLINA, SIT-INS

Constitutive Publics and the Role of Audience

Richard W. Leeman

The rhetorical elegance of the lunch counter sit-ins has been widely and appropriately noted. As historian George Lewis summarizes, "the dominant analytical view continues to be that much of the sit-ins' success was predicated upon the ability of protestors to juxtapose outward displays of their own morality and higher purpose with the base racism and impatient, febrile violence of their segregationist foes."[1]

Although the sit-ins were elegant in their ability to reify within a single act the aspirations of African Americans and the oppression of segregationists, the rhetorical power of the demonstrations were not drawn solely from the juxtaposition of peaceful college students with puerile White segregationists. Indeed, local reactions to the lunch counter sit-ins varied from community to community, as the case studies of Charlotte and Rock Hill exemplify.

In Charlotte, North Carolina, the sit-ins began on February 9, 1960, were suspended in March when the city formed an interracial committee to address the issue, resumed in early July when little progress had been made, and were resolved shortly after that, on July 9. During the Charlotte sit-ins, three arrests of demonstrators were made resulting in two convictions totaling $15 in fines, with no reports of physical violence against either protestors or White resistors. In Rock Hill, located just thirty miles away from Charlotte, on the South Carolina side of the state line, students from Friendship College began occupying lunch counters the day after the Charlotte protests began. In Rock Hill, however, there were persistent reports of "tension," arrests were frequent, no city commission was formed, and a year later in the spring of 1961 the protestors resorted to a "Jail, No Bail" strategy to force the city's hand. The rhetorical strategies and tactics used by the lunch counter sit-ins in the two cities were remarkably similar. The contrasting audience reactions, however, resulted in strikingly dissimilar rhetorical events.

Such diverse reactions were not surprising because, despite the popular stereotype, Southern Whites were divided in their opinions on the issue of race. One manifestation of those differences is found in White segregationists' attacks directed toward other Southern Whites: "When White Citizen's Councils emerged [following the Brown decision] it was soon obvious that they were as committed to stamping out dissent among white southerners as they were dedicated to the intimidation of local black activists."[2] Urban economic centers such as Charlotte were often described as "progressive" and had acceded to token school integration by the time of the lunch counter sit-ins.[3] Rock Hill, in contrast, was a large rural town situated in the state that had led the South's secession in 1861, and ninety-nine years later it was still steeped in Confederate lore. Its commitment to segregation ran deep. In response to a 1957 bus boycott, for example, the Rock Hill Bus Company discontinued routes through Black neighborhoods, even at the cost of going out of business the next year.[4]

The audience, as Chaim Perelman and Lucie Olbrechts-Tyteca remind us, is a critical element in the rhetorical process: "For argumentation to develop, there must be some attention paid to it by those to whom it is directed."[5] Although the rhetor may broadly conceptualize a universal, or idealized audience, the rhetorical act is ultimately directed toward what Perelman and Olbrechts-Tyteca formulate as the *particular* audience, that is, "the ensemble of those whom the speaker wishes to influence by [the] argumentation."[6] The rhetor believes these auditors will react "rationally," that is, in predictable ways and open to persuasion. No matter how large the ensemble, however, every audience is composed of individuals, and it is to each that a rhetor must speak. As Kenneth Burke argues, persuasion occurs through the process of identification. A rhetor persuades "only insofar" as the rhetor's and auditor's ideas, images, attitudes, and language are "identified" with one another.[7] Identification occurs only when the rhetor's and audience's perspectives are conjoined, or consubstantial, with each other.[8] Rhetors cannot force such identification. Through their discourse and their actions, they can only offer its possibility to each member of the audience. It remains for the audience to complete the act of identification, and thus be persuaded.

What James Boyd White calls a "textual community" emerges through this process of identification.[9] Although persuasion begins with what may be termed a "text"—in this instance, the lunch counter demonstrations—if the "text" succeeds, the audience will "become a community among many readers of the text," specifically constituted by those "who will adopt its terms and methods and use them to achieve their purposes in the world."[10] To achieve "active belief, commitment and participation" of the audience, the rhetor and audience must construct "structured ways of thinking and talking" so that the audience will "see things in the world as [the rhetor] presents them in [the] text—to think and to feel about them as [the rhetor] does," and thereby "form a community."[11] Identification is attained and the rhetorical act is completed only through the formation of this kind of discursive or "textual" community.

In this essay, I argue that the lunch-counter demonstrations and the accompanying rhetorical statements in Charlotte by Whites as well as African Americans constructed a constitutive public that was able to dominate the discourse. Although an oppositional public did resist, their voice was muted and rhetorically marginalized. In Rock Hill, however, no similar discursive community coalesced around the lunch-counter demonstrations. Instead, the White segregationist public was able to preserve its dominant voice, and thus maintain a rhetorical division between the races. The sharply divergent discursive communities which were constituted in these two cities invited sharply divergent outcomes.

Charlotte

On February 2, 1960, four African American students from North Carolina A & T University sat down for service at the Woolworth's lunch counter in Greensboro. Twenty-two-year-old Charles Jones, a student at Johnson C. Smith Theological Seminary (JCSTS), was riding home to Charlotte from Washington, DC. when he heard the news on his car radio. He recalled his elation at thinking that this was the spark that was needed in the civil rights movement, and upon his return to Charlotte he and several other students called a meeting to consider whether a similar sit-in should be conducted in Charlotte.[12] At JCSTS, approximately 650 students met the evening of the 8th and approved joining the "movement." The following day, some 260 students forced the closing of eight lunch counters in downtown Charlotte.[13]

The Students' Text

From the very start of the demonstrations, the *Charlotte Observer* framed the demonstrations in terms that were faithful to the students' intent. In the first article reporting the Greensboro sit-in, the story quoted one student who summarized the issue as one of fundamental fairness: "They sell us merchandise from the other counters. If they sell us other merchandise, we say they should serve us at the lunch counters."[14] The newspaper's day-two coverage of the sit-ins quoted a student who grounded the issue on the nation's bedrock ideals, as he paraphrased the Declaration of Independence: "As American citizens, we believe and know all men are equal. . . . If the employees, Caucasians and ne-groes, can work together, shop together, why can't they eat together at the same luncheon counter?"[15]

As the Charlotte sit-ins began, the *Observer* similarly underlined the princi-ples enunciated by the Johnson C. Smith students. Fundamentally, the issue was characterized as one of fairness and basic human dignity. Blacks were served at all the other department store counters, and "there is no discrimination until we sit down at the food counter."[16] "I have no malice, no jealousy, no hatred, no envy," Jones was reported as saying, "all I want is to come in and place my order and be served and leave a tip if I feel like it." As with the newspaper's earlier reporting on the Greensboro sit-ins, an appeal to American ideals was quickly introduced, as Jones observed that the lunch-counter sit-ins were "parts of my race's efforts to secure God-given rights."

Throughout its reporting of the Charlotte sit-ins, the *Observer* reiterated these two elements of the students' message, and thereby helped the students' text "emerge." On the one hand, the issue was cast as one of fairness. Receiving service at the lunch counter, said Jones, "is important to us only insofar as we in Charlotte happen to agree with the great thinking of history, that every individ-ual in the world has been endowed with basic human dignity."[17] Another of the student leaders was quoted as observing that "we're not seeking intermarriage. We don't feel that sitting next to a White person will help us digest our food any better. We just want to be able to sit down and have a cup of coffee like other customers."[18] As Jones summarized succinctly, "we are asking only for the right to walk upright like a man."[19] Again, however, appeals to the ideals of America and Christianity were interwoven with these more fundamental requests for human dignity. When Charlotte's mayor asked students to abandon the protests in the name of "preserving good relations" between the races, the students re-sponded that, while they did not want to damage race relations in the city, "we feel, however, that we must continue our effort to achieve the recognition of hu-man dignity that rightfully belongs to every person and, as citizens, to enjoy the same privileges as any other customer or citizen of this growing community."[20] Photographs of demonstrators' signs similarly captured the dual message of ba-sic human rights and the rights of American citizens. The three signs pictured carried the slogans "Prejudice is the Child of Ignorance," "Justice: Do You Know the Meaning?" and "Not Separate, Just Equal."[21] When the *Observer* reported on a March 13th rally held at Gethsemane A.M.E. Zion Church, it noted that the meeting included the singing of "America" and "Onward Christian Soldiers."[22]

On February 20th, the students suspended their sit-ins when the mayor suggested that meetings between the students, restaurant managers, and city leaders could be called. When those meetings failed to materialize, the students resumed their protest. On the 20th, however, when they announced the cessation, they also released a statement that detailed their case for the sit-ins. That statement was published in its entirety in the *Observer*. In the message, the students asked first to be treated fairly, like any other human being: "Fair play does not say that citizens of the Negro race can be served at counters one, two, three four and five, but not at counter six because counter six happens to sell food and drink."[23] Their argument implicitly asked the audience to apply the Golden Rule, and asked how Whites would feel to be treated the way African Americans were: "To see total strangers from every corner of the earth enter our community and be afforded the use of all public facilities while these public facilities are denied to fourth and fifth generation Southerners is a searing experience." Significantly, the statement asserted the students' claims as Southerners as well as Americans, thus constituting themselves and the audience as comembers of the community twice over. They explicitly rejected the claim that non-Southerners were involved in the protests: "It will not serve the continued prosperity of this great city to forward rationalizations and pretexts such as 'They were prodded by outside influences,' and 'They are happy only the NAACP puts ideas into their heads.'" "Nothing more is involved," the statement read, "than the privilege to walk upright as citizens of this community." Interestingly, while basing their claims on their status as citizens, the students leapfrogged the broad rights asserted in the Declaration of Independence and Constitution, and instead invoked British common law as it pertained specifically to public accommodations: "Service is a public right which stretches back into early Anglo-Saxon law governing innkeepers." The statement culminated with a nod towards the students' and audience's shared religious heritage, prophesying that future observers would praise Southern Blacks for their "adherence to Christian principles and [their] sense of humor," concluding that "the goal can be delayed; [but] it cannot be denied for much longer."

In addition to adopting the students' frame from the onset—the lunch counter sit-ins as an effort to secure fairness and their God-given/American rights —the *Observer* emphasized the peaceful and disciplined nature of the protests as well as the civility of White Charlotteans. "The students themselves," the paper reported, "were orderly and several of them said they had experienced no abuse from store employees or bystanders."[24] "In all cases the students were quite orderly" the paper reported on February 11th; police had told them not to block the aisles, and so they kept moving.[25] The students have "conducted themselves with remarkable dignity and restraint" the paper editorialized on the 15th, and the paper's reporting continued in that vein throughout the protest.[26] Kind words from the students were also faithfully and routinely reported, as when the demonstrators issued a statement that said they appreciated the Charlotte police conduct that week, and that "we are very fortunate to have such police here in Charlotte."[27]

For their part, student leaders consistently accentuated the positive. In March, Jones assured reporters that "tension isn't high" in Charlotte, because "we feel a majority of the white community has identified itself with our movement. We get these feelings from the statements of church leaders, telephone calls, letters to the papers, and the actions of community leaders."[28] Instead of violent confrontation, he said, the lunch counter sit-ins in Charlotte had resulted in "a heck of a lot more communication between the races" and "if only this is accomplished it will be a tremendous amount of good."

Two significant rhetorical features emerge from this narrative—one that was carefully cultivated by the students and faithfully reported by the *Observer*.[29] First, it was the African American protestors who bore witness to the city's reasonableness. In contrast to the heckling, chaos, and arrests being reported across the region from Raleigh to Nashville, Charlotte's decorum and civility were being certified by the students themselves. There was, implicitly, a sense of civic pride in how the city was conducting itself. Second, the students' peaceful and orderly conduct was reported by the paper as intentional on the part of the protestors. In their planned meeting the evening before the sit-ins began, the paper reported, students had agreed that "we want to be orderly, we want to be peaceful, we want to be served."[30] The "remarkable dignity and restraint" that the protestors subsequently displayed was therefore not accidental. From the very start, the Charlotte student protestors were portrayed as intelligent and well-disciplined, a stark contrast to the common stereotype of African Americans held by many Whites.

This positive image of the student protestors was enhanced in part by Charles Jones's appearance on the front page of the *Charlotte Observer* two days before the Charlotte sit-ins began. On February 5th, Jones had testified before the House Un-American Activities Committee (HUAC) regarding his attendance and public debates at a recent student leadership conference held in Vienna, Austria. The conference, sponsored by the Soviet Union, had been an obvious attempt to proselytize to Western students the virtues of Communism. At the conference, Jones had vocally defended the ideals of the American political system as well as its possibilities for change. Jones had sharply rejected Paul Robeson Jr.'s allegation that Black Americans were still "slaves," saying that to so characterize them diminished the gains Blacks had made through hard work and diligence, although there were "plenty of things to be improved about the Negro's status in the U.S."[31] For obvious public relations purposes, the HUAC invited Jones to share the story of his international defense of the United States, which Jones gladly did, although they abruptly halted the testimony when Jones noted that, as an African American, "it's much easier to be an anti-Communist than it is to be a good, responsible American."[32] Some members of the HUAC were disturbed by that "turn" in Jones's testimony, and the committee abruptly took a recess and declined to hear any more testimony from Jones. Several members of the committee, however, including the chair, apologized to Jones for the behavior of the others.[33] Significantly, the tenor of the *Observer's* front page story was that Jones had been thoughtful, forthright, and principled in his defense of America, and in its subsequent coverage of the Charlotte sit-ins, the newspaper reminded its readers of Jones's recent testimony and his "articulate" defense of the United States in an international setting.[34]

The Community's Response

Although the newspaper's reporting positively reinforced the students' message, its editorial policy was much more cautious. In its first editorial on the subject, on February 15th, the *Observer* did compliment all sides for their good behavior. Students, law enforcement, and lunch-counter managers "have conducted themselves with remarkable dignity and restraint."[35] The editorial distinguished, however, between "tax supported" segregation—e.g., public schools—and segregation as practiced by private establishments: "One is a matter of individual legal rights which transcend race or color; the other is a matter of individual choice." Business owners were entitled to conduct their affairs in any manner of their choosing, the editors asserted. Also, civil disobedience was still disruptive of the public order; no matter how well behaved the participants. "From the first," wrote the editors, "we have regretted the Negro students' choice to pose this particular issue at this particular time," since Blacks have enjoyed support for legal rights from "many white Southerners" and, the paper hinted ominously, "may risk alienating" that support. Here was a "moderate" editorial line that would be echoed by many newspapers, business leaders, and government officials throughout the South. Five days later, the *Observer* repeated its argument, coupled with an appeal that a committee be formed to discuss the matter. Students had made their point "with dignity and persuasiveness," the editorial opined, but merchants were "quite right" that they had "a right to conduct their business as they please."[36] Police had conscientiously maintained law and order. A conference may produce nothing, but should "at least be tried." The question at hand was a pragmatic, not moral, one. Merchants should look at other parts of the country to see if "continued segregation of lunch counters has cost Negro patronage or whether desegregation has cost white patronage."[37]

However, while the newspaper's official voice supported order and stability over principled stands, readers were treated to a steady drumbeat of public endorsements from the community for the students' campaign. Although much was made in an early report that Nathaniel Tross, publisher of the Black-owned

Charlotte Post, had condemned the sit-ins as "ill advised," the impression quickly emerged in the *Observer* that Tross was an outlier and that the Charlotte African American community uniformly supported the students. Their demonstrations were quickly endorsed by the president of Johnson C. Smith Theological Seminary as well as its faculty.[38] On February 10th, Kelly Alexander, local community leader and president of the state chapter of the NAACP, announced that the association "endorsed unequivocally the orderly protests."[39] On February 16th, two more African American organizations, the Women's Auxiliary of the Charlotte Medical Society and the Baptist Ministers Conference of Charlotte, announced their support.[40] Two weeks later, the Johnson C. Smith alumni association publicly supported the students. "We are American citizens," the association's statement read, "and [we] deserve all the rights of all other citizens of this free country."[41] On March 12th, the community hosted a rally at Gethsemane A.M.E. Zion Church, where one of the meeting's leaders, Dr. Givens of Biddleville Presbyterian Church, concluded that "believing that basic human dignity is a thing inherent in all mankind, we support the student protest movement wholeheartedly."[42] The students' sit-ins, Givens said, represented the "struggle against inequality and injustice," and as such enjoyed the full support of Charlotte's African American community.

The African American community's united front was an important message in this case. White segregationists often claimed that most African Americans were "content" with the order and stability of the South and that those who protested the current system were only the troublesome "few." The unrelenting message in the pages of the *Charlotte Observer* was that the African American community in Charlotte was *not* content with the status quo and that those Blacks sitting at the lunch counters represented *everyone*, whether young or old, middle class or poor. The students were not alone.

Nor was the African American community alone. Just as consistently as the *Observer* reported endorsements by local African Americans, it featured reports of support by White leaders and organizations. Three days after the protests began, the North Carolina Council on Human Relations and the Unitarian Fellowship for Social Justice endorsed the demonstrations. Writing on behalf of the latter, Dr. Sydney Freeman, pastor of the Charlotte Unitarian Church, asserted that "we believe that the Negroes are acting from religious conviction and are conducting themselves with dignity."[43] On February 21st, the Evangelical Christian Church of North Carolina announced that it "thoroughly approves" the sit-ins because it wants "all people, regardless of color or race to receive equal treatment."[44] Ninety-five percent of the association's members, the spokesman said, were White.[45] On February 27th, the Charlotte Society of Friends argued that Whites in the city should "practice the Christianity we preach and the Negroes are now using."[46] On March 15th, the Mecklenburg (County) Christian

Ministers Association passed a resolution that "it is our conviction as Christian ministers that discrimination on the basis of race must ultimately be brought to an end." The Association urged "all citizens of our community to endeavor sincerely to make valid the Christian ideals of human dignity upon which our nation was founded."[47] The Association further pointed out, and the paper reported, that there had been 160 members present at the meeting and that "there was no opposition" to the resolution.

As remarkable as this parade of endorsements by local White associations was the virtual absence of organized White opposition, at least as reported in the newspaper. No White Citizens' Councils, no Charlotte chapter of the Ku Klux Klan, and no ministerial associations materialized locally to condemn the protests. The organized opposition was reported, but those groups were always situated as outsiders: e.g., the North Carolina State Baptist Convention, North Carolina Association of Quality Restaurants, the Greensboro Ku Klux Klan.[48] Even when reporting on the Black community meeting at Gethsemane in March, the *Observer* made a point of reporting on the comments made there by an "elderly white woman." She had attended the recent trial of three protesters who had been charged with misdemeanors, and said that it was clear from the trial testimony that the Blacks at the demonstrations had "conducted themselves far better than the whites had."[49] What emerged was the impression that the Black community in Charlotte unanimously supported the students' goals, and that they enjoyed broad support within the White community as well.

The *Charlotte Observer's* "Letters to the Editor" during this period wove an equally intriguing narrative. Across the two months of active protests, letters written by self-reported White citizens in support of the sit-ins were lengthy, articulate, and cogently reinforced the students' arguments. In contrast, letters published in opposition to the sit-ins were less frequent, shorter, and often awkwardly written. In the language of the day, the "better class" of Whites was portrayed as supporting the students' goals, while those opposed represented the other "elements," many of them from outside the city.

Sit-in supporters agreed that segregated lunch counters were unjust. "As a Southerner," wrote one woman, "I share in the guilt of perpetrating such invidious, nondemocratic traditions. It is not a question of law, for laws can and should be changed. The question, it seems to me, is one of justice."[50] "Segregation has produced a tremendous amount of injustice in this country,"[51] observed another writer, and penned another: "Segregation is a dead end for Southern progress. . . . [I] urge the stores to recognize the justice of [the Negro students] plea."[52] Another writer argued that the demonstrations constituted a wake-up call for Whites to recognize Blacks as "men": "We do not see that in exerting our superiority we are flagrantly displaying our ignorance."[53] Writers also echoed the ironic unfairness that the students had enunciated from the start: "At many of these lunch counters, Negroes may serve but they cannot be served. At other counters in the same store, they can buy but they cannot sell."[54]

Another theme developed in these letters echoed Edmund Burke's aphorism that the only thing necessary for the triumph of evil is for good men to do nothing. Lunch-counter discrimination is "unjust, unnecessary, and unwise," wrote one, and those who cooperate in that are "just as guilty as if committing the crime."[55] Others extended on his argument. "Can one stand by and ignore human injustice?" asked one letter writer.[56] Others answered: "[I] agree with [the first letter writer] that to not raise one's voice against wrong is to participate in the evil."[57] And another: "I think now is the time for all people of good will and integrity to do something about a wrong that needs to be righted."[58] Indeed, to readers who followed the opinion pages of the newspaper, the distinct impression was that White residents of Charlotte recognized that the student sit-ins had brought the inequities of segregation into sharp relief and galvanized the White community into finally standing up for justice. "I am an average Southerner," asserted one writer, who recognizes that "my fellow Charlotteans [simply want] equal facilities"; it is time for Charlotte and North Carolina to take "one more step forward in the right direction."[59]

White letter writers also recognized the hypocrisy of professing American democratic ideals while discriminating against Blacks on an institutional basis. "We profess to be a democracy with liberty and justice for all," lamented one, "while we relegate an entire racial group to second class citizenship."[60] Others agreed: "this is a request I feel they should not have had to make. It should have been their rightful privilege all along."[61] From this perspective, letter writers recognized African Americans as full citizens of the country, entitled to all the rights and privileges that would attend that citizenship. Demonstrators were to be "commended for their courage" in asserting those rights, because "in this great country of ours, we are all created equal."[62] The Constitution and Bill of Rights had been "slapped" by segregation, and such practices needed to desist.[63] "Let us provide opportunities to all American citizens," wrote another, so that all may "understand each other better."[64] The student demonstrators had founded their actions on their rights as American citizens. As portrayed in the Letters to the Editor, most White Charlotteans fully agreed with that claim.

The students had also asserted their "God-given rights" in the matter, and here, too, the White community concurred. White letter writers frequently encouraged fellow Whites to apply the Golden Rule. Put yourself in "the position of the Negroes," urged one, while another chided that "We are being very obtuse in not placing ourselves in the position of the Negroes to understand their real objectives."[65] Another writer explicitly claimed Scriptural authority: "Where in the Holy Bible [does he find] any support for racial discrimination? I have yet to find in my Bible anything that I would interpret to mean that anyone, simply because his skin pigment contains more pigment than mine, should be treated as an inferior, and denied rights taken for granted by me."[66] Argued another, "the true and living God is the creator and maker of all men and He makes no mistakes!"[67] Another pointed up the irony that the Reverend Billy Graham was currently conducting revivals on the continent of Africa, while the descendants of Africa in "the South [find themselves] in pursuit of the happiness, freedom, and dignity guaranteed under the Constitution."[68] Thus there emerged a "textual," or discursive, community that coalesced around the students—sharing a common language and values that constituted a community dedicated to treating African Americans as full-fledged citizens endowed and entitled to be treated with the dignity, respect, and rights that such status implied.

In contrast, the letters of those opposed to the lunch-counter sit-ins were brief, less eloquent, and more often listed an address that placed the letter writer outside Charlotte. The most common defense focused on technical legalities, rather than larger notions of political good or moral right. The lunch-counter sit-ins were simple "lawlessness," wrote one, and a South Carolina reader asked rhetorically, "What intentions the Negroes of North Carolina had except to cause trouble and create disturbance?"[69] To admit that a disturbance was being caused, however, validated African Americans' claim that they were being denied rights that they wanted to have, and so a few writers attempted to shift the blame to outside agitators, especially the Communists. Claimed one, "I think the movement is communist inspired."[70] Another similarly argued that "the socialists push integration."[71] Weighed against the letters which specifically alluded to the language of the Declaration of Independence and Constitution, these vague assertions sounded hollow. It did not help their argument that the leading spokesman for the students had publicly rejected Communist ideology in national and international settings just weeks before the sit-ins. Nor did the claim of "lawlessness" seem to take hold when news reports and many letter writers remarked that "what the students are doing is orderly."[72]

Probably the most rhetorically persuasive argument presented by opposition letter writers centered on the "free right of association." On the one hand, letter writers could attempt to ground the "principle" in pragmatics: e.g., "you can't force it (association) on people."[73] Most also tried to situate the claim legally, and associated the argument with god terms such as "rights" and "democracy," and thereby counter the proponents' claims that the political principles of liberty, equality and human dignity were at stake. There are the "rights" of the individual to "pick his own associates" and "rights of proprietors to serve or not serve," and asked another, "does [democracy] not give a business the right to set its own policies?"[74] "Democracy is a two way street," asserted another, and "forcing rights is like asserting right-of-way in driving."[75] Still, taken holistically these letter writers sounded petty and petulant when juxtaposed with those who appealed to the dignity, equality, and fair treatment of all people. Sit-in supporters also rebutted their opponents on principles of law: "A state license is not 'private. . . . [The presence and conferral] of city, county and state licenses means it's a public business and everyone is invited, [so] 'come all the world.'"[76]

Few letter-writing critics of the lunch counter sit-ins explicitly defended segregation. The few who did trotted out the well-worn responses. One of those was fear of the "slippery slope." "Moderation" on race would just lead to more demands: "You have to stop any thing before it gets started. We must not allow integration in any form."[77] Significantly, there was a plea to stop integration without any justification or defense of segregated society. The author simply assumed that readers would have the same perspective. Given the discourse that was filling the news and editorial pages, however, it was a naive rhetorical stance at best. Another letter writer baldly appealed to prejudice in defense of segregation. "Would [the] white supporters of the demonstrators invite a Negro into their own home?" he asked. The answer, he assumed, was "no," and it would be their "right" not to, and store owners also have that "right."[78] His assertion, however, was belied by the facts. Before the lunch counter stools had been removed and Blacks blocked from entering the cafeterias, some Whites had offered Blacks their seats, and in the middle of the demonstrations some White church members of St. Peter's Episcopal Church downtown invited two of the student leaders to join them in their Wednesday noon meal, and the students had accepted the invitation.[79] Within the Charlotte community, then, Whites *would* sit down and eat with Blacks, and the letter writer's claim was thus implicitly invalidated. The anachronism of these few rhetors who defended segregation was perhaps best demonstrated by the letter written by a self-identified "94-year-old man" who wrote that what was at stake were the "bedrock principles and vital interest in both races," because the "segregation of the races is absolutely the only way for the two races to live together and prosper."[80] In an age of television, air travel, and satellites, the "voice" of segregation had been born in 1866.

Constituting a Discursive Public

For those readers who embodied Perelman and Olbrechts-Tyteca's notion of the universal audience, the debate as conducted through the *Charlotte Observer's* "Letters to the Editor" pages tilted sharply in favor of the demonstrators. Letters in support of the sit-ins were more substantive, framed squarely within the auspices of the country's founding documents as well as Christian principles, and had a distinctly modern flavor. The *Observer's* formal editorials hewed a middle line, but its Letters to the Editor page did not, and a question arises as to where the newspaper's allegiance truly lay. Some contemporary observers argue that the tilt in favor of the sit-ins found in the hard news stories and letters represented the editor's agenda to further desegregation.[81] Charles Jones told an interesting story in this regard. During the period of the demonstrations, the night editor at the *Observer* took to calling Jones in the evening anytime there was a sit-in story that would be running the next day. The editor called in part to both verify the accuracy of the story and ascertain Jones's and the students' point of view regarding whatever angle of the story was being covered.[82] The practical result was that the students were fully conversant with the substance and direction of the paper's news coverage, and the newspaper was fully apprised of the students' arguments and perspectives. Indeed, Jones specifically recalled that the *Observer's* coverage of the sit-ins was generally "objective" and "factual," and, most importantly, it provided the community with coverage of the demonstrations that allowed people to make their own informed opinion.[83]

The night editor's telephone calls were not the only tangible sign of support the students received from Whites in the Charlotte community. From the beginning, Jones's understanding was that the mayor and city council had instructed the police not to do anything "stupid" that would exacerbate the situation and cause more trouble. Early on, a group of young Klansmen drove in from Monroe, North Carolina, a town just to the east of Charlotte, to see what trouble they could raise at the sit-ins. According to Jones, the Charlotte police chief took some pleasure in recounting the story, telling Jones how the police had met the Monroe Whites at the Belks department store, rounded them up, and then dropped them back off at the county line with the instructions "don't bring yourselves back up in here."[84] Tensions did rise at the end of February, as protesters "charged that some policemen had 'pushed' them around, used abusive language, harassed some of them with unwarranted traffic tickets and refused to permit them to swear out warrants against White persons who assaulted some of them."[85]

The city council immediately issued a statement that said it had not approved such tactics and forwarded the complaints to the chief of police. The police chief reasserted the principle that the mission of the force was to "enforce the law impartially." The students asserted that "recently" there had been incidents and released a list of four specific occurrences but concluded with a bridge-building statement that "the police force has conducted itself in a commendable manner protecting the rights and property of merchants and all persons involved." Significantly, further incidences and tensions were not reported, suggesting that there was substance to the students' compliment that Charlotte was "fortunate" to have such police.[86] While the conduct of the police force was not beyond reproach, both the students and city leaders accentuated the positive, reinforcing the points of agreement rather than division.

In a similar manner, influential White citizens reached out to support the students. Sydney Freeman invited Jones to speak to the Unitarian congregation. After Jones's talk, church members asked if they could be allowed to join the students in their campaign.[87] Another memorable instance was an invitation to dine at a private residence in the upscale Myers Park neighborhood, arranged by Harry Golden, publisher of the *Carolina Israelite*. The invitation came from Mrs. Cannon, widow of one of the Cannon textile magnates. Jones and another student leader went uncertainly to the dinner, not sure what to expect. What they found were several other prominent White citizens from Charlotte, including one of the only women office holders in the city. The discussion, Jones said, began with their White hosts listening and questioning the students, as the White leaders sought to better understand the students' point of view. What ensued at this and subsequent meetings at Mrs. Cannon's house became what Jones termed a "forum," one which created a "comfort zone" between these White leaders and the students. Another discursive bridge that emerged was humor. When two light-skinned African Americans were inadvertently served at the Liggett's lunch counter and then walked out to join the students' picket line, Harry Golden jokingly suggested that perhaps the department stores needed to install a "pigment meter" so that they could tell who "should" and "should not" be allowed service. Jones believed that some Whites' ability to laugh at their community's foibles and prejudices provided important rhetorical room for change to occur. The result of all this was that, in Jones's recollection, the student demonstrators enjoyed a "broad base of support within the [Charlotte] white community."

Jones also attributed the success of the Charlotte sit-ins to the unanimous support of the African American community. As with the tangible signs of White support from community leaders, the impression that the Black community supported the students was manifested in many ways. According to Jones, faculty and administration talked with students to provide them guidance and encouragement. Ministers exhorted the women of their churches to boycott the downtown department stores. Students regularly heard words of encouragement and congratulations from the business and community leaders. When the city experienced three major snowstorms in late February and early March, the finest cars in the community—including Cadillacs from the local funeral homes—showed up to shuttle the protestors downtown and back. Jones also recalled his "eyes and ears" at meetings of the mayor, city council, and business leaders—African American servants who waited on these city leaders as they discussed the sit-ins. Jones vividly recollected the excitement in the African American maid's voice in July, when she called him to let him know that the department store owners had agreed to serve Blacks at the lunch counters. "We did it, didn't we, Mr. Jones!" she told him, and her use of the first-person plural spoke of the community's solidarity. Before the announcement was ever made public, Jones and the others knew all the details of the protest's resolution.

On July 9, 1960, sixteen days before Greensboro reached a similar conclusion, the City of Charlotte announced that its lunch counters would be integrated. The protests had been conducted with few arrests, almost no fines, and no reported violence. Much like their counterparts across the region, the students had astutely fashioned their rhetorical message, but it is also important that their message had found a fertile audience in Charlotte. City officials and business leaders favored an image of progress and the cultivation of business over the continuation of traditions of segregation. The African American community was fully supportive. The mainstream newspaper accurately conveyed the students' message, and its letters to the editor gave the impression that the thoughtful and principled majority of Whites in Charlotte supported the lunch counter demonstrators. Through this interaction of texts was constituted a public that dominated Charlotte's rhetorical landscape; a discursive community that constructed a language of shared values; and norms that explained, justified, and enabled the peaceful integration of the city's lunch counters.

Rock Hill

In Rock Hill, the White community's response to the protests was different from the onset. On February 12th, the first day that students from Friendship College went to sit-in at four lunch counters downtown, Whites reacted swiftly and aggressively. The protests began around 11 a.m. and by 1:30 p.m. it was reported that all four lunch counters had closed. The students conducted their protests using the same rhetorical strategies as their compatriots in Greensboro, Charlotte, and elsewhere. The *Rock Hill Herald* did note that the students were "orderly, polite, well-dressed and quiet": "Nearly all the young Negro boys wore suits and ties. The Negro girls also were neatly dressed. They were polite and quiet and did not talk much, even to each other. Many of them opened books and read as they sat at the counters—school textbooks, Bibles, and workbooks. One girl was reading a book entitled 'The Liberty of God.'"[88] In the initial span of two and one-half hours, however, crowds of Whites "gathered on sidewalks and in stores," a thrown egg "hit a Negro in the head," and an "ammonia bomb" was set off, which caused "tears to flow freely" for a few minutes.[89] At Woolworth's, it was reported that "white hecklers were able to provoke no response from the Negroes. One youth harangued them for around an hour," but the students did not answer the jeers and taunts. Despite the protestors' polite and orderly conduct, however, the immediate and intense reaction of Whites in Rock Hill was summarized in the anecdote of "a gray haired little woman [who] went up and down the line of seated Negroes with bitter remarks about being unable to eat there like every day."

Constructing the "White" Text

Initially, the *Rock Hill Herald* downplayed White reactions by reporting that "for the most part, curious adults, white and Negro, . . . took no part and gave no hint of violence or aroused feelings."[90] Similarly, the paper merely allowed that the bomb threats, ammonia bomb, and thrown eggs "could be related to the demonstration," as if some alternate causality to the disturbances might eventually be uncovered.[91] Despite these descriptions, which downplayed the protests, the newspaper's headline read that "Negro Youth *Invade* RH Lunch Counters" (emphasis mine), and the lunch counter demonstrations across the South were labeled a "strike" in this staunchly antiunion state.[92] Furthermore, the newspaper immediately raised the specter that outside agitators lay at the root of the city's troubles, as it passed along without question the "unconfirmed report that a number of cars bearing North Carolina license plates and Johnson C. Smith stickers were seen in Rock Hill this morning."[93]

White resistance to the demonstrations continued as the dominant theme. On the second day of protests, Rock Hill "tensed" for confrontations, although the demonstrations were canceled due to a snowstorm.[94] However, Woolworth's and McCrory's had removed lunch counter seats in preparation. "No trespassing" and "Restaurant closed" signs had been posted around the counters, and a group of White people had gathered to pass out slips of paper asking Whites to boycott any lunch counters who would allow Blacks to remain on the premises, even if they had been refused service. Their notices were inelegantly written, however: "Please do not make a purchase in this store until further notice. The white citizens." When these White counterdemonstrators realized that their plea could be misconstrued as *supporting* the Black protestors, they quickly discontinued. Although the White community's impromptu reactions had been swift, certain, and overwhelmingly negative, resistors were unwilling to continue relying on chance. "There were solid reports," said the *Observer*, "that some white citizens are rallying behind organized efforts to counter the Negro demonstrations."

Unlike the Charlotte community, where opposition was sporadic and actively muted, Rock Hill's resistance to the protests was organized and authoritative. The York County Citizens' Council worked quickly to rally opposition around two central themes: maintaining law and order, and resistance to outside "encroachments" on freedom. Four days after the protests began, a "crowd of 125 persons" was told by "a top Citizens' Council Leader" that the Citizens' Council could "deal with Rock Hill's racial problems" by relying on

South Carolina law.[95] The *Herald* reported that the Council believed it had taken "up the cudgel against hate and violence," and "a good Christian, intelligently planned course of action in immediate racial issues was endorsed."[96] The South Carolina Segregation Committee similarly argued that "further invasions of private eating establishments . . . were bound to lead to unpleasantness and tensions."[97] However, the Committee asserted that the protests offered the community an "excellent opportunity" to prove that segregation can be upheld in "a lawful and peaceful manner."[98] In its open letter to the public, the Citizens' Council congratulated itself for having recognized that "if violence was to be avoided, something had to be done immediately" and for having acted on that impulse. The leaders had gone to the government to insist that the laws be upheld, and, asserted the letter writers, "thanks to these men, [the Citizens' Council leaders], Rock Hill is quiet and segregated."

The *Rock Hill Herald* added its authoritative voice to warn about the dangers of turmoil and praise the virtues of order. In an editorial on February 18th, the *Herald* called the Citizens' Council "a welcome voice of restraint," saying that Farley Smith, executive secretary of the state organization "urged law and understanding in a time of tension."[99] The editorial ignored the protestors' principles, writing simply that the "Negro students demonstrated against segregated eating practices in public areas." "Think what you will of the White Citizens' Councils," the newspaper wrote in a bid to appear objective, but Smith's words "probably did much toward wetting the fuse of an emotional powder keg. And it could be that people of both races owe him a debt of gratitude."

"Freedom of association" was the second prong of the organized resistors' argument, a theme often distilled to the simple term "freedom" and then expanded to encompass the Cold War rhetoric of American freedom versus Communist dictatorship. Within this frame, the demonstrations were not simply a matter of integrating lunch counters at the local five-and-dime store. As the Citizens' Council argued, "our fight is not a fight between races, not a fight between creeds, not a fight between sections, . . . but a fight between tyranny and freedom. This is America's fight."[100] The sit-ins, they argued, threatened to undermine the American way of life. This meant, of course, that "foreign" and "outside" instigators—such as those from North Carolina and Johnson C. Smith Theological Seminary—were to blame. "It's been said we use the word Communism too loosely," Smith allowed at a mid-March meeting of the Citizens Council, "but all this is categorically Communist-inspired. You are told the lunch-counter sit-downs were spontaneous, but they blew up everywhere."[101] In a March 14th letter mailed to some 2,000 residents in the county, the Citizens' Council warned that organizations with "high sounding names" were nothing more than pressure groups "to foster foreign ideologies by further spreading hatred and mistrust among our people."[102] "Now you have scalawags among you," the Council warned, resurrecting the Reconstruction-era pejorative for Southerners who cooperated with the Northerners after the Civil War.[103]

Although the *Herald* did not explicitly lay responsibility for the protests on outside agitators, it did cede merchants with the legal and moral authority to decide the matter and joined that argument of freedom with the need to maintain order. In late February, a *Herald* editorial observed that lunch counter owners had three options: serve Whites only, serve Blacks also, or "get rid of lunch counters."[104] The store owners' decision, the paper said, was "squarely up to them." That decision was "overdue," however, and "the longer management of the stores delay their decision the longer the city will be subjected to tensions and a deterioration of relations between the races." Implicitly, race relations had been peaceful and amicable before the lunch counter protests. The bus boycott of 1957 was blithely ignored.

In addition to the organized citizen's councils and the local newspaper, government officials were supportive of the Citizens' Council's arguments and prosegregation position. All seemed to agree that the purpose of the sit-ins was to make trouble and upset the natural order but not to gain rights. Early on, South Carolina Governor Ernest F. Hollings denounced the demonstrations, saying that they were "purely to create violence and not to promote anyone's rights."[105] Like the Citizens' Council, State Senator L. Marion Gressette also blamed the unrest on outsiders, saying that the sit-ins were "instigated by outside agitators who have no interest other than creating racial disturbances." Rock Hill Mayor John A. Hardin more broadly cast the issue as one of disturbing the established order and therefore the city's "peace." He quickly asked the stores for a "definite policy" because "the continued state of indecision is creating a hazard on Rock Hill's main street."[106] Although explicitly defining the community's norms would presumably "help" restore equilibrium, the onus for the disturbances lay solely with the students: "It is my hope that no further demonstrations will take place. I request all citizens to exercise their civic responsibility and seek a return to normalcy."[107] Within the sweeping appellation of "all citizens," the Black college students were targeted. It was, after all, their sit-ins that lay at the root of all the "demonstrations," and a "return to normalcy" would require a return to honoring segregated lunch counters, the very norm the students were trying to overturn in the first place. Like the *Herald,* Mayor Hardin portrayed pre-protest race relations as having been harmonious and desirable. "Law and order" thus meant the laws of second-class citizenship and the order of segregation.

As if the current laws were not up to the task of returning the state to normalcy, however, South Carolina legislators proposed new laws that would ensure the maintenance of "order." One bill drafted and proposed on February 17th provided for fines up to $100 and jail up to 30 days for trespassing at eating establishments. A second measure would allow stores to institute a "cover charge" for anyone seeking service, although payment of the cover charge would not guarantee that the payee would receive service.[108] By early March, it was reported that there were five new bills pending in the South Carolina legislature that were designed to stop the sit-ins. One bill would allow municipalities to revoke the health certificate of lunch counters whose "practices . . . caused or could cause public disorder or provoke civil strife."[109] Thus, any lunch counter owner who instituted a "definite policy"—to use Mayor Hardin's words—that *allowed* integration could have their health certificate revoked because such integration could be termed a "practice" that caused public disorder or provoked civil strife. It was not *any* "order" which the "law and order" advocates in South Carolina sought but the order of normalcy, the status quo, and segregation.

Citizens, leaders, and government officials did not simply talk to one another in back rooms or through the media. On February 25, for example, Gressette and State Senator Robert Hayes attended a meeting of the York County Citizens' Council. Now, however, the issue *was* a matter of "rights." "No one," declared Gressette, "can be forced to serve anyone in his place of business whom he does not wish to serve. The trespass law is clear."[110] Here was a further radicalized perspective that moved beyond the argument for general order and stability, instead dividing the participants into two camps—those who were in the moral right and those in the moral wrong. "There is no middle ground," Gressette was reported as saying, "You are either for segregation or against segregation." He congratulated the "citizens councils" for standing up on behalf of what was "right," as well as for their "sound leadership," and the *Herald* faithfully recorded that Gressette received a standing ovation at the conclusion of his remarks.[111]

Maintaining the Rhetorical Divide

Not only were the government officials' and citizens' melodies consonant with one another but also the entire band seemed to occupy the same marching field, and there was no discursive space for the player who thought that democratic, humanitarian, or Christian principles were at issue. On March 16th, Governor Hollings attacked President Eisenhower's speech on race and rejected his proposal that states establish biracial committees to negotiate a satisfactory conclusion. The president, Hollings argued, did not realize that "these incidents are explosive," a condition that he claimed was probably exacerbated by Eisenhower's meddling. Hollings gave a dire warning that "these situations have moved from a consideration of rights to a consideration of maintaining peace and good order," an ironic warning since a month earlier he had declared that the sit-ins were not a matter of principles or rights.[112]

Of course, Hollings's statement that the president was fanning potentially explosive flames also gave the lie to the Citizens' Council's declaration that sound leadership and maintenance of the status quo has resulted in a "quiet and segregated" Rock Hill, but then anyone paying the slightest attention to Rock Hill knew that while the city had indeed remained segregated, it was hardly quiet. Even with lunch counters temporarily closed to "wait out" the sit-ins, students and their opponents gathered outside the stores. On February 15th, the city was "the scene of near-incidents" as "White youths harassed Negroes outside."[113] The next day, bands of White youth and Black youth were reported milling about the streets and, while there were no reports of physical violence, "dog chains, tire tools, and knives" had been sighted.[114] On February 23rd, the lunch counter sit-ins resumed. Almost immediately upon the protestors' arrival, the counters closed. The students returned to Friendship College, but when news arrived that the counters had re-opened quickly upon their departure, they returned to downtown. The cat-and-mouse game continued, and the lunch counters closed once more. An estimated 200 people gathered outside the stores, with Whites "jeering [at] the Negroes" and police continually cutting a path through the crowd. Only African Americans, however, were arrested. One protester was arrested for "breach of peace," and another was taken into custody for his "own protection . . . after a crowd of white persons began chasing him."[115] Faithfully adhering to the White community's narrative that the sit-ins were the work of outside agitators, the *Herald* reported that "the six Negroes who entered Woolworth's stepped out of an automobile bearing a North Carolina license plate."[116] The next day, White youth showed up early to the lunch counters to occupy all the seats before the Black students could arrive. These White counterdemonstrators would then carefully "swap out" their seats only to other Whites. When three Black students managed to gain seats at the counter, one of those was "pulled" from the seat by White youth. A "brief scuffle" broke out "between white and Negro youths," and then "police rushed in and dispersed the crowd."[117] On February 29th, a robed, but unmasked, Klansman visited the lunch counters.[118] On March 15th, seventy protestors were arrested. The demonstrators had marched in front of City Hall and sat-in at two bus stations and one drug store.

Where Charlotte demonstrators were able to make a point of congratulating the city police force for its restraint, the NAACP publicly criticized the "strong arm, fascist-like tactics of the peace officers" in Rock Hill. Like their Charlotte counterparts, the Rock Hill students' leader indicated that they "would welcome any negotiations," but none were forthcoming.[119] As the NAACP noted in mid-March, responsible White community leaders had shown "no inclination to hear the students' grievances or to seek a democratic solution," which was reflected in the pages of the *Rock Hill Herald*.[120]

Muting the Students' Voice

Rhetorically, no student protest text was allowed to emerge around which the larger community's discourse might coalesce. Only once during the protests did the newspaper give full voice to the protestors' principles of freedom and equality. A March 1st news story covered the previous day's community meeting held at a local Black church. The thrust of the meeting was to discuss a boycott of Rock Hill stores in support of the lunch counter protests. Two major arguments emerged. First, that the protests were an issue of rights and equality. Said one spokesman, the demonstrations "are for the purpose of securing equal rights for all through passive resistance. . . . Discrimination in itself is wrong. . . . It makes a white man feel superior; it makes the Negro feel inferior."[121] Second, attendees asserted that outside "agitators" had nothing to do with the protests; dissatisfaction with segregation began at home. Said T. E. Murdock, a photographer who was documenting the sit-down protests, Rock Hill Blacks should write the stores' management and "tell them we in the South are dissatisfied. They are being told in the North that we Negroes are satisfied with conditions. They are saying these demonstrations are brought on by outside agitators. We are intelligent enough on our own." The Reverend C. A. Ivory, a recognized leader in the Rock Hill African American community, summarized both rhetorical themes: "The history of the South is a list of repeated abuses against the Negro. They've lynched us. They've passed all kinds of silly laws to keep us in check. . . . [They say we're outsiders, but] these are home people. [Any foreigner] can eat with whites and there are no questions about it. But here I am, born in America, but because I am a Negro, I can't do it. It doesn't make sense." Once aired, however, the students' rhetorical text was quickly consigned to journalistic exile, never to be heard from again.

Several letters to the editor supported the protests, but none was allowed to enunciate the principles of equal rights explicitly. One, by an AME Zion minister, observed that "we as ministers preach from the same kind of Bible" and that "from one man came all the families of the earth."[122] He also noted White Americans' double standard: "We as a group often hear such words as these, 'The Negro should stay in his place.' It puts us on the spot. When we ask where is our place, there is no answer. When war comes [however], the Negro's place is in the Army to fight for his country." One letter by self-identified White South Carolinians argued on behalf of African Americans' right to peacefully protest and objected that "to arrest a group acting in a non-violent protest because some "other" group MIGHT BECOME VIOLENT seems to us a restraint upon the wrong citizens."[123] The rhetorical effect of this letter was undercut, however, because three times the letter writers analogized the student protests to the right of unions to demonstrate—that is, to strike—a comparison not likely to have won many converts in Rock Hill, South Carolina. The one other White-authored letter in "support" of the protests simply disavowed the White counterprotestor who had appeared in Ku Klux Klan regalia, and asked, "can we not do them [the student protestors] the courtesy of negotiating with them on the level of their obvious maturity and peaceful intentions?"[124]

Constituting a Resistive Community

The newspaper's "conversation" on the topic is interesting here. Only African American voices were heard enunciating the principles on which the demonstrations were founded, and even then only rarely. White voices in support of the protests were minimized by being aligned with organized labor or restricted to asking for "negotiations" and "peace." White segregationist voices, however, were given free rein: "I am a white citizen of York County but I do not consider myself superior to any person because of his race, creed, or color. However, I am proud of my race and intend to do everything in my power to keep my race as pure as God has made it. . . . [Merchants would benefit from the boycott because] generally speaking, the Negro trade in these stores consists of large crowds in the aisles with very little money being spent."[125] Beyond the letters to the editor, a far larger platform in the news-story section was provided to White organizations, such as the Citizens' Council, and to elected government officials. Members of these groups and government officials asserted the community's right to "freely associate"; that their troubles were being caused by outside agitators and Communists. They also asserted the need to encourage law and order so that the community could return to "normalcy."

Two editorials in late March evidence the public that was constituted by the *Rock Hill Herald's* discourse. On March 24th, the newspaper asked, "Why Don't the Silent Speak?" In this editorial, the newspaper characterized the debate as one being carried on by the "extremes": "The integrationists speak out often. So do the segregationists. And they take the position that you must belong in one camp or the other. You are not allowed any middle ground."[126] "Few things," the paper opined, "are that simple. Especially the complex, heart-rending subject of race relations." Although the newspaper's discourse had now moved away from congratulating the Citizens' Council as a "welcome voice of restraint," it refused to acknowledge—even implicitly—the student protestors' principles. Instead, the issue was cast purely as a matter of "change," which integrationists would like faster and segregationists would like slower. Race relations was still portrayed as a problematic issue that threatened the peace and was best left to the community—a rhetorical body politic constituted by the discourse of the segregationists and not by that called forth by the vocabulary of the students or African American leaders. "In the delicate area of race relations," the *Herald* averred, "there are more than two sides. There are many sides." The *real* Rock Hill community belonged, "for the most part, in the grey area between the two extremes." The change would come, but it must come slowly and carefully, within the bounds of law, order, and *normalcy*.

The *Rock Hill Herald* cemented that discursive position four days later, as it reprinted an editorial from the *Wall Street Journal*. Here was a national, Northern-based newspaper's editorial—published under the bald headline "Some Racial Facts and Fallacies"—which certified the language and values that constituted the discursive public that the Citizens' Council, government officials, and *Herald* had evoked. First, the *Journal* reported, "the Negro has come remarkably far, politically and economically, in the past hundred years."[127] Thus, the pace of change in the South was endorsed as reasonable. Second, the North had no business intruding on Southern racial relations, because "the discrimination and segregation which still widely exist is not a Southern monopoly." Third, and perhaps most importantly, although "the Negro is entitled to the rights and protections the law provides other citizens," it was "a misreading of human nature to suppose that divergent cultures can be forced into harmony." Freedom of association was both a right as well as a matter of pragmatics, and "legislation which goes beyond ensuring equality before the law and seeks to compel immediate social integration is doomed to failure." "Such enforced togetherness," the *Journal* wrote, if passed, "amounts to regimentation, *an invasion of individual rights*. And, as a practical matter, it is likely to acerbate rather than alleviate race relations" (emphasis mine). The protestors' claim of right to be served in a public place of business is silenced here, while the segregationists' claim of right to associate is announced and endorsed. The editorial concluded by confirming the *Herald's* discourse that change will come but must come slowly to guarantee law, order, and peace: "That may be part of the trouble in the South today: too many people have been trying to push the goal of harmonious race relations too far too fast. The past hundred years show that spectacular progress in race relations can occur. But zealotry will only retard improvements."

The Friendship College students had conducted their sit-ins by using the same rhetorical appeals as had the Johnson C. Smith theology students in Charlotte but with entirely different results. A year later, the demonstrations were still dragging on when the Rock Hill students decided upon a "Jail, No Bail" strategy because paying their fines and bail was, as Charles Jones put it, a "game" that the White "power structure of Rock Hill was playing."[128] The dominant voice of the Rock Hill community was that of Whites who supported the status quo and characterized the student protest as a threat to law and order. The Rock Hill students' text was never allowed to emerge in any substantial form, and thus no broader, alternative community was constructed whose language and values contested the segregationists' rhetorical ground. As discursively constituted in public forums, Whites in Rock Hill were not willing to listen to what the protestors were saying. In Charlotte, they were.

Conclusion

When asked in an interview why the Charlotte community was open to lunch counter reform, Charles Jones focused on two elements: money and leaders in the White community who were willing to speak out for change. As he recalls, there was no mistaking that race prejudice existed in the community. When the lunch counter sit-ins began, Jones heard on good authority that the owner of Ivey's Department Store swore he would shutter his business before he allowed the counters to be integrated.[129] By July, however, between the sit-ins and the African American community's general boycott of the department stores, the stores' very existence was being threatened. The lunch counters must be integrated or there would be no stores in which to have the counters. A national chain such as F. W. Woolworth's might survive, but the locally owned Belk's and Ivey's would not.[130] Where the Rock Hill Bus Company owners had been too willing to close their business rather than desegregate, Belk's and Ivey's were not. Money also played a role more broadly. Charlotte considered itself a "progressive" town, focused on business, growing its financial reach, and chasing Atlanta as the Southeast's hub of economic activity. The lunch counter sit-ins were visual and visceral. This sort of racial conflict would not play well with investors, clients, and markets located outside the South. When tensions did flare during the sit-ins, the City Council moved quickly to reprimand the police and reassert the need to resolve the issue peacefully. "Peace" was not defined as a synonym for "law and order," as it was in Rock Hill. Charlotte was a business city, Jones recalled, and it was less interested in maintaining segregation than it was in doing business. Racial unrest did not pay well for anyone.

In addition to such monied interests, however, Charlotte had leaders in the White community who were willing to speak up and tangibly act in support of the students, and what emerged was a discursive community that bridged, at least in part, the rhetorical division between the races. Religious organizations publicly endorsed the students and their goals, leaders in official and unofficial capacities reached out to the students, and letters to the editor created a culture of thoughtful agreement with the democratic principles being espoused by the students. Additionally, in Charlotte's discursive milieu, the citizens allowed students' voices to be prominently heard. Their stated positions were regularly reprinted and in full. Not only were their principles fully consonant with the White voices read in the letters to the editor but also the students' discourse was regularly validated by the published compliments that the demonstrators were principled, disciplined, and thoughtful. In Charlotte, therefore, a discursive community emerged, which employed the language and values that allowed Whites to identify with Blacks and the protestors' frustrations, perspectives, and aspirations. Indeed, Whites in Charlotte were not simply able to identify with the Blacks' cause but were repeatedly invited to do so.

In contrast, a discourse of division dominated the Rock Hill White community's response. African American voices were marginalized, while the White majority was discursively constituted as a public who believed that the student protestors were troublemakers, rather than principled demonstrators. Government officials, organizations, and the common person on the street vocally and repeatedly rejected the students' claim to equal status and a citizen's privilege. The values of "law and order" and "normalcy" drove Whites' discourse, and the students' sit-ins were visually and inherently not "normal." The government's focus was not on constructing a common language of rights and democratic values, but rather on how institutions could prevent "them" from disturbing the status quo. Rather than build bridges, the White community's discourse sought to plug the dam. Negotiations could not take place, as the two discursive communities—White and Black—were talking qualitatively different languages. Protestors were arrested, and no integration of the lunch counters took place. In May of 1961, as the Freedom Rides commenced from Washington, DC, it is perhaps not surprising that the first bus station at which riders were assaulted was in Rock Hill.[131]

For Perelman and Olbrechts-Tyteca's universal audience, and the public that was constituted in the Charlotte community, the lunch counter sit-ins were compelling rhetoric. Eating food is an archetypal human activity, and the African American youth were seeking a simple repast when they sat down to be served. The rejection they faced reified the discriminatory practices of segregation, demonstrating the deep division that existed between the treatment of Whites and Blacks solely by skin color. The juxtaposition of Black college students and their quiet dignity, with the heckling abusive language and behaviors of Whites—often uneducated—further illustrated the injustice of segregation.

It only did so, however, because a significant portion of Charlotte's White community moved to seek identification with the Black students. Such Whites were ready to listen, be moved, and to act upon their motive for identification. This is not to say that the city was free from racial disturbances led by Whites or that the City of Charlotte did not drag its feet through desegregation. However, there was a body of rhetoric that constituted a sufficient public that dominated the White Charlotte community's discursive response, and ultimately there was negotiation from which emerged integrated lunch counters.[132] As Charles Jones recalled there was a "profound difference" between the two cities' reactions to the lunch counter sit-ins, and the majority of the particular audience in Rock Hill's White community were not similarly moved.[133] Here, neither students' texts were given a full and sustained voice nor did a White voice emerge that could coalesce with that of the students, bridge the rhetorical divide, and constitute a discursive public with shared language and values. Rock Hill Whites did not linguistically identify with the Black students who sought basic lunch service and therefore discursively reinforced the racial divide rather than bridged it. The consequences were very different in Rock Hill, as violence and tensions forced Black protestors to adopt the "Jail, No Bail" strategy in 1961, and spring of 1961 saw more physical violence as the Freedom Riders bus protest moved through Rock Hill. The rhetorical act is inherently collaborative, and the nature of White citizens' collaboration with the African American lunch counter protestors was radically different in Charlotte, North Carolina, than it was in Rock Hill, South Carolina. A rhetorical drama so effective in one location with one particular audience fell largely on deaf ears just thirty miles south.

Notes

1. George Lewis, "Complicated Hospitality," 41.
2. George Lewis, *Massive Resistance*, 10. See also 9.
3. Bartley, *The New South*, 140, 220.
4. Ibid., 181.
5. Perelman and Olbrechts-Tyteca, *The New Rhetoric*, 18.
6. Ibid., 19.
7. Burke, *A Rhetoric of Motives*, 55.
8. Ibid., 20–23.
9. White, *When Words Lose Their Meaning*, 193.
10. Ibid.
11. Ibid.
12. Charles Jones, personal interview, December 6, 2013.
13. Ibid. In the *Observer*, the number was put at 200. See Covington, "Negroes' Protests Close Local Diners."
14. "Negroes Seek Diner Service," A6.
15. "Negroes to Stay Til Served," A8.
16. This and the following quotations in the paragraph are from Covington, "Negroes' Protests Close Local Diners."
17. Covington, "Students Hope to Talk it Over."
18. Covington, "'Sitdown' Is Explained By Students."
19. "Students Seek Aid of Negro Adults."
20. Covington, "Smith University Students Suspend Demonstrations," B1.
21. Munn, "Negro Demonstrators Wave Money and Signs," D1.
22. "Students Seek Aid of Negro Adults," B1.
23. This and the following quotations in the paragraph are from "Students' Viewpoint in Protest," A14.
24. Covington, "Negroes' Protests Close Local Diners."

25. Covington, "Negroes Continue Protest at Diners," A1+.

26. Covington, "Negroes Continue Protest at Diners"; Claiborne, "41 Raleigh Negroes Arrested in Protest for Food Service"; and "Lunch Issue No Public Affair," B2.

27. Claiborne, "41 Raleigh Negroes Arrested in Protest for Food Service."

28. This and the following quotation are from Oberdorfer, "Negroes Expect Integrated Cafeteria," B1.

29. Jones noted in his interview that Charlotte student leaders paid close attention to emphasizing the *why* of the demonstrations, rather than the what, how or where, and that they were deeply committed to demonstrations that would be dignified and nonviolent. Jones, personal interview.

30. Covington, "Negroes' Protests Close Local Diners."

31. Oberdorfer, "Charlottean's Debates Stun Red Hunters"; and Jones, personal interview.

32. Oberdorfer, "Charlottean's Debates Stun Red Hunters"; and Jones, personal interview.

33. Jones, personal interview.

34. Covington, "Negroes Continue Protest at Diners."

35. This and the following two quotations are from "Lunch Issue No Public Affair," B2.

36. This and the following quotation are from "A Conference Is In Order Now," B2.

37. "A Conference Is in Order Now." Later editorials continued in the same vein. See, e.g., "Let's Seek Lunch Counter Peace," B2.

38. Covington, "Negro Protests Close Local Diners." Tross was clearly isolated, however, when the next day Johnson C. Smith theology students hung the publisher in effigy. Although that demonstration was condemned by the sit-in leaders, Tross recanted his opposition and later supported the sit-ins. See Covington, "Negroes Continue Protest at Diners" and Covington, "Students Hope to Talk It Over."

39. "Students Hope to Talk It Over."

40. "Negro and White Youths Stage Fight in High Point," B1.

41. "Smith Alumni Backing Students," B2.

42. This and the following quotation are from "Negroes 'Explain' Today," B2.

43. "Students Hope to Talk it Over."

44. "Evangelical Church Approves Sit Down," B2.

45. Ibid.

46. "Protests Possess Gandhian Character," B2.

47. This and the following quotation are from "Ministers: Racial Fight Must End," B1.

48. "Baptists Against Negro Protests," A3; "Negro Group Backed," B1; and "Klan, White Youths Vie for Seats With Negro Students in Diner Protest," A3.

49. "Students Seek Aid of Negro Adults," B1.

50. "World Is Seeing Injustices in Stores," B2.

51. "Demonstrations Reveal Symptoms," B2.

52. "Does the South Have Peculiar Sadism?" B2.

53. "Negroes Are Right," B2.

54. "Moral Integrity and Lunch Counters," B2.

55. "Stores Are Not Restaurants," B2.

56. "Democracy Isn't for a Few People," B2.

57. "Intolerance Shows One's Inferiority," B2.

58. "Good Will Stands at Lunch Counters," B2.

59. "Charlotte People are Enlightened," B2.

60. "The Lunch Counter Dollar is 'Different,'" B2.

61. "Thinks Everyone Should be Served," C2.

62. "The Demonstrators are U.S. Citizens," B2.

63. "Everybody Wants to Be Accepted," B2.

64. "Understanding Leads to Race Harmony," B2.

65. "Pride or Principle in Lunch Question?" B2; and "Charlotte People are Fair Minded," B2.

66. "Hefner's Bible Not Like Hers," B2.

67. "God Isn't Color Blind," B2.

68. "Students Pursue Goals At Home," B2.

69. "Everyone Loses in the Sit Down," B2; and "Students Cause Trouble," B2.

70. "Color Lines in North," B2.

71. "The Socialists Push Integration," B2.

72. "Robeson Affair Quite Different," B2.

73. "Brother 'Rock' Earned His Welcome," B2.

74. "Cool Heads Should Not Be Rushed," B2; and "Democracy is a Two-Way Street," B2.

75. "Forcing One's Rights Can Be Disastrous," B2.

76. "State License is not 'Private,'" B2.

77. "Some Questions in Race Relations," B2.

78. "Integration is Matter of Mind," B2.

79. Covington, "Negroes Continue Protest at Diners"; and "Two Negroes Eat at White Church Here," C1.

80. "Sentiment Can't Solve the Problem," B2.

81. See, e.g., Flono, "Helping Charlotte Find Its Way—50 Years Ago."

82. Jones, personal interview.

83. Ibid. In contrast to the much larger *Observer,* Jones recalls the *Charlotte News* as being overtly racist in its coverage.

84. Ibid.

85. This and the following two quotations are from Joe Doster, "Negroes Protest City Police 'Manhandling,'" B1.

86. Claiborne, "41 Raleigh Negroes Arrested in Protest for Food Service."

87. Quotations and details in this and the following paragraph from Jones, personal interview.

88. "Negro Youth Invade RH Lunch Counters," *Rock Hill (SC) Herald,* 1.

89. This and the following two quotations are from Snook, "Four Rock Hill Stores are Hit By Protest," A2.

90. "Negro Youth Invade RH Lunch Counters."

91. Wilder, "Two Rock Hill Lunch Counters Close; Seats Removed, Drug Stores Re-Open," 1.

92. "Negro Youth Invade RH Lunch Counters"; and "Negro Students Strike Lunch Counters," 1.

93. "Negro Youth Invade RH Lunch Counters."

94. This and the following quotations in this paragraph are from Shaheen, "Food Counter Protest Canceled By Weather," B2.

95. Shaheen, "Citizens Council Unit Planned at Rock Hill," A3.

96. Caldwell, "Citizen's Council Leader Urges Law, Not Violence," 1.

97. "Students Continuing Lunch Counter Drive," A7.

98. This and the following two quotations are from "'Separate But Equal' Plan Upheld."

99. This and the following two quotations are from "A Welcome Voice of Restraint," 4.

100. Caldwell, "Citizen's Council Leader Urges Law, Not Violence."

101. Davis, "Meet Disappoints Citizens' Leaders," 1.

102. "'Separate But Equal' Plan Upheld," 10A.

103. Davis, "Meet Disappoints Citizens' Leaders." One should remember that in 1960 the Civil War was *still* known among many White Southerners as the "War Between the States" or, even less diplomatically, as the "War of Northern Aggression."

104. This and the following two quotations are from "A Decision is Needed But Overdue," 4.

105. This and the following quotation are from "Students Continuing Lunch Counter Drive."

106. Shaheen, "Mayor Asks Policy on Lunch Counters," B1.

107. Ibid. See also "Hollings Has No Comment On Report," 1.

108. "S.C. Bill Would Halt 'Sit-Down' Movement," A7.

109. "S.C. Bills Would Nip Sit-Downs," A5.

110. Wilder, "600 Hear Gressette Push Citizens Council," 1. See also Shaheen, "Law Can Stop Negro Protests, Senator Says," B1.

111. Shaheen, "Law Can Stop Negro Protests, Senator Says"; and Wilder, "600 Hear Gressette Push Citizens Council."

112. Wickenberg, "Hollings Hits Ike's Race Talk," 1A; and "Students Continuing Lunch Counter Drive."

113. "Fighting Erupts During 'Protest,'" A1.

114. "Negro and White Youths Stage Fight in High Point."

115. Shaheen, "Negroes Resume Rock Hill Protest," C1.

116. "Lunch Counter Sitdown Resumes in Rock Hill," 1.

117. "Whites, Negroes Scuffle in Some Areas," B4.

118. "Chapel Hill Scene of Negro Protests," A15.

119. Shaheen, "Negroes Resume Rock Hill Protest," C1.

120. Heffner, "Hundreds Arrested as Negroes Protest," A1.

121. This and other quotations in this paragraph are from Davis, "Rock Hill Negroes Threaten Boycott."

122. This and the following quotation are from "The Negro Needs Answers for Questions," 4.

123. "They Protest Arrest of Demonstrators," 4.

124. "The Contrast Was Painful," 4.

125. "Negro Boycott Wouldn't Hurt Merchants," 4.

126. This and the following quotations in this paragraph are from "Why Don't the Silent Speak?" 4.

127. This and the following quotations in this paragraph are from "Other Folks Say: Some Racial Facts and Fallacies," 4.

128. Jones, personal interview. In support of the Friendship College students, Jones participated in the Jail, No Bail sit-ins and served thirty days at the York County prison farm, including a stretch in solitary because he and another student refused to stop singing spirituals.

129. Jones, personal interview.

130. Ibid.

131. Lewis, *Massive Resistance*, 137–138.

132. There were indeed lawsuits, marches, and even some firebombing. In May 1963, the city finally moved assertively to desegregate all public accommodations and held "eat-ins," which paired White and Black community leaders who then went to dine together at the "White tablecloth" restaurants. See Washburn, "Hawkins' Way—and Charlotte's—Helped Restaurants Integrate," and Flono, "Helping Charlotte Find Its Way—50 Years Ago."

133. Jones, personal interview.

VISUAL NARRATIVES, CHRISTIAN RHETORIC, AND *KAIROS*

The New Orleans Woolworth's Sit-In

Lesli K. Pace

On September 9, 1960, the first lunch counter sit-in held in the city of New Orleans took place at Woolworth's Department store on Canal Street at Rampart. Though the United Defense League had organized a bus boycott in Baton Rouge in 1953, the New Orleans sit-in organized by Rudolph "Rudy" Lombard, a civil rights activist and member of the Congress of Racial Equality (CORE), set the stage for future sit-ins and led to the integration of New Orleans lunch counters in 1962.[1] Nearly a year later, on June 11, 1963, President John F. Kennedy made explicit the ethical and moral components of extending the same rights guaranteed for White Americans to Black Americans by referencing well-known religious teachings. In his "Civil Rights Address" he said, "We are confronted primarily with a moral issue. It is as old as the Scriptures and is as clear as the American Constitution. The heart of the question is whether all Americans are to be afforded equal rights and equal opportunities, whether we are going to treat our fellow Americans as we want to be treated."[2] Though Kennedy's appeal differed in that it was made by a president and presented to the nation as a whole, members of the civil rights movement had long made this claim to local and regional audiences. Activism rooted in religious ideologies, supported by churches, and carried out by those with faith characterizes the sit-ins that took place across the decades and make Christian rhetoric a compelling way to approach analysis of the sit-ins. As Leonard Gadzekpo asserted, "The core values of black culture—such as freedom, justice, equality, an African heritage, and racial parity in all aspects of life—were inherent in the black Christian ethos that gave birth to and nurtured the civil rights movement."[3]

As Aldon Morris argued, the sit-ins of the 1960s were crucial to the development of the civil rights movement "because their rapid spread across the South crystalized the conflict of the period and pulled many people directly into the movement."[4] As was noted in the introduction to this volume, much has been said about sit-ins as a form of nonviolent protest, but few scholars have focused on sit-ins as uniquely rhetorical, and even fewer have examined lesser known sit-ins. Existing research recounts personal experiences as a "sit-inner," examines why individuals chose to participate in sit-ins, and investigates the repercussions of differentiation in protest strategy.[5] This research laid the foundation for future scholars to explore the value, strategies, and implications of sit-ins as a form of social protest.

For this chapter, then, I draw on notions of Christian rhetoric and its close counterpart *kairos*[6] to explore the rhetorical implications of three images: images that echo broad-reaching cultural ideologies and occur in a unique moment in time. More specifically, I argue the images captured during the first lunch counter sit-in that took place in New Orleans draw on a locally powerful understanding of Christian moral code and Christian visual rhetoric to invite the audience to support racial integration. Although civil rights sit-ins share commonalities across space and time, each is also unique. Thus, I highlight the implications of the location, time, culture, and participants to more fully understand how the New Orleans sit-in interpolated local community members as well as people across the United States.

Christian Rhetoric

During the second sophistic and as Christianity began to take hold in Rome, rhetoricians faced considerable resistance from Christians who perceived the practice as focused primarily on the attainment of self-interests.[7] Augustine of Hippo, a rhetorician who converted to Christianity, ushered rhetorical theory into the realm of Hebraic discourse that focused on notions of the divine thus aiding the acceptance of classical rhetorical practices in Christian teachings. The relationship between traditional rhetoric and Christian rhetoric is not difficult to recognize since it shares the same foundation. For example, George Kennedy argues that Aristotle's theory of rhetorical proof—especially ethos, logos, and pathos—are apparent in Hebraic discourse but carried different meanings because the rhetor is the focus in Aristotle's theory, whereas God is the focus in the Hebraic tradition.[8] As Christine Mason Sutherland explains, "it is His [God's] reliability that certifies the truth of the message, not that of the prophet himself. Similarly, the speaker does not invent, or find the message: that is given by divine revelation."[9]

To bridge this divide and demonstrate the value of rhetoric for clergy and other members of the Christian church, Augustine shifted the focus of rhetorical theory from being rhetor centered to being audience centered. He did this partly in response to the work of Cicero and Quintilian by contending the rhetor should seek to enlighten rather than persuade the audience. In *On Christian Doctrine,* Augustine offers guidance as to how Christian rhetors can encourage "psychological and social order by correctly interpreting the Christian truth of the Scriptures and conveying this truth to diverse audiences."[10] Further, Augustine argues that rhetoric should be used for the good of the people and suggests three duties of the rhetor: to conciliate the hostile, arouse the careless, and inform the ignorant.[11] In each case, Augustine urges the rhetor to focus on the needs of the audience.

Sutherland posits that by the time Augustine wrote the fourth book of *On Christian Doctrine*, he was nearing the end of his life and had moved beyond his focus on truth, which was characteristic of his early Neoplatonism, and had fully developed his own theology. She argues that Augustine's theology was firmly grounded in his "principle of love" and made clear "that our relationships with other human beings—our neighbours—are dependent upon, integrated with, our relationship with God."[12] Sutherland also contends that Kenneth Burke's notion of identification, division, and consubstantiation, which are informed by Augustine's theory of Christian rhetoric, highlight the ways being charitable can shape the relationship between rhetor and audience.[13] Where Cicero positioned rhetors as more powerful than the audience and prepared them to face resistance to persuasive appeals, Augustine suggested a balancing of power between the audience and rhetor and highlighted the ability of the audience to actively engage the message. In these ways the rhetor and audience find commonalities (identification), even in the awareness of their differences (division), and they can seek to come to a different understanding and state of consciousness through the process (consubstantiation). Sutherland wrote, "It might even be said that the supreme act of identification—the equalizing of the sender and the recipient—is the incarnation: here indeed the divine humility brings itself down to a level at which communication becomes possible in an entirely new way."[14]

Kairos

Though it is a concept with contested meaning, a general understanding of *kairos* entails noting that an expression of time (chronos) is intrinsically connected to context and will be evaluated by its appropriateness (decorum or fitness) or lack thereof.[15] It indicates a rhetorical moment that is possible only because it happens in a specific chronological time and in a precise location with the appropriate people who are acting in the ways that are necessary. William Trapani and Chandra Maldonado argue that *kairos* accounts for the way rhetors "engage in practices that not only adapt to and shape their spatial-temporal vectors but inaugurate conditions that may wholly redefine those eras so that they are no longer 'of a piece with itself.'"[16] Trapani and Maldonado's claim is essentially that there are moments, specific instances in any given time period that come to represent the whole of that era, and to understand the era and the people living in it we must be aware of and make sense of these moments. Further, Trapani and Maldonado's effort to consider a more contemporary understanding of materialistic rhetoric leads them to theorize *kairos* as an element of metistic rhetoric, a rhetoric that sits at the intersection of being and becoming. They note that metis positions knowledge as emerging from malleable and changing situations, thus metistic rhetoric becomes an "interrogation of thresholds of sensibilities, including those that span constitutions of human, animal, machine, the ecological, and their myriad combinations."[17] As each of these intersect with one another, *kairos* becomes a way to explore the "transformation" rhetors experience as they make "dynamic and reflexive" choices that "exhibit inventive resourcefulness" and impact protests on "both global and individual scales."[18]

Whereas Trapani and Maldonado's approach highlights the implications of identity, cultural constraints, and the involvement of calculated risks, Ian Bekker posits that *kairos* "implies a sensitivity to the contingencies of a particular context" and is linked to *phronesis,* which he defines as "practical wisdom" through *paideia* or "the education of the citizen."[19] This shift in understanding emphasizes not only the qualitative aspect of time but also the impact judicious discourses have on shaping the knowledge and understanding an audience has of that moment. Bekker goes on to explain that, "kairos calls for appropriate behavior in terms of both local and non-local contexts. . . . [Non-local contexts] refer to broader, 'congealed', repeatable structures on an ethical, linguistic, and social level, [while local contexts] demand a suitable, potentially unique, response to the exigencies of an immediate context."[20] Further, Bekker asserts that *kairos* is connected to Christian rhetoric through contextual and liberation theologies. These theologies emphasize that biblical passages must be interpreted within the context they were written and should be outside political, social, and economic oppression. Both are rooted in ethics and are "reflected by its emphasis on orthopraxis as opposed to orthodoxy."[21] The distinction between these two terms is key. While orthodoxy expresses the long-standing traditions and beliefs of groups or sects, orthopraxis emphasizes action in response to social injustice. More specifically, orthopraxis is the convergence of theory and practice, and in the context of Christianity, is focused on the actions of the believer resulting from their religious ideologies. Thus, Bekker argues "it is only at certain opportune moments (i.e., *kairoi*) that the Prophetic Spirit is able to break 'through the barriers of the law.'"[22]

A Uniquely Louisiana Sit-In

In his discussion of the history and development of civil rights movements in the United States, Paul Wehr claimed that, rather than think of the various eras and generations of activism "as a single social phenomenon evolving through successive phases" it is more accurate and productive to acknowledge that they are in fact "a cluster of sub-movements, each developing out of a peculiar set of conditions with its own leadership, ideological orientation and tactical approach to goal-attainment."[23] Louisiana, a territory colonized by the French in 1682, purchased by the United States in 1803, and admitted to the union in 1812, is a state unlike any other in the country. Diverse ethnic groups have shaped the values and practices of Louisiana through the food, music, culture, and laws, echoing this eclectic heritage. Given the cultural diversity of New Orleans and the public statements made by local officials, a common misconception exists about race relations in the city during the civil rights movement of the 1960s. Anna Marcum wrote that the perception of New Orleans as a place that is "leaps and bounds ahead of the rest of the South" is a myth "perpetuated by the city's mayor at the time, deLesseps Story 'Chep' Morrison," who claimed New Orleans had "good race relations" after an on-campus protest of segregation took place at Dillard University. Morrison claimed that White government officials were working to "create and maintain a climate for the realization of greater economic opportunity . . . within the framework of existing State laws and customs," which in this context meant following Jim Crow segregation laws.[24] Positioning the resistance to integration as the result of city official's investment in protecting the economic health of the city, rather than being rooted in blatant racism, was a unique ploy that skirted the morality and ethics of integration by focusing on the economy.

Often thought of as the epicenter of the state, New Orleans is regularly the site of firsts in Louisiana. In 1960 nearly 40% of the population in New Orleans was Black. Three prominent historically Black universities—Dillard, Xavier, and Southern—located in New Orleans, provided a bevy of potential sit-inners because many participants in sit-ins were college students. Given the demographics of New Orleans, the practice of segregation was even more blatant than in cities with fewer people of color, but it was also better primed for action. In fact, many New Orleans citizens had practice with nonviolent direct action. Because the largest shopping district in New Orleans, which was on Canal Street, consisted of shops owned by Whites who refused service to Black customers and prevented White Jews from owning stores, members of the Black and Jewish communities developed a second shopping district on Dryades Street, which locals referred to as the "Black shopping/commercial district."[25] Ironically, even on Dryades many of the shop owners were White Jews who would sell products to the Black community but refused to hire Black people for "white jobs" such as clerks and managers. Toward the end of 1959, New Orleans civil rights leaders formed the Consumers' League of Greater New Orleans (CLGNO) and tried to negotiate with Jewish business owners, expecting them to be more understanding since they too experienced discrimination. When nothing changed, the CLGNO organized a boycott that took place the week before Easter in 1960. Although it was normally one of the busiest shopping times of the year, the stores and streets were empty. As one can imagine, this had a huge impact on the stores in this district, but rather than change their hiring practices, most stores closed their doors and moved to the White suburbs.[26] This degree of White flight is indicative of just how fully instantiated racism and segregation were in New Orleans. Here, again, the nature of New Orleans created a unique situation that movement members had to effectively navigate if there was any hope of seeing changes.

The situation in Louisiana was also unique because there were no official segregation laws, only local custom. In fact, in *Lombard et al. v. Louisiana*[27] the court found that the "pro-segregation statements of Mayor Chep Morrison 'achieve[d] the same result'" as if there had been laws on the books.[28] Chief Justice Earl Warren wrote the opinion for the court and concluded, "These convictions, commanded as they were by the voice of the state directing segregating service at the restaurant, cannot stand."[29] In other states where official laws and ordinances were on the books protestors had concrete changes to make. In Louisiana, movement members had to determine the best way to change customs, beliefs, and practices and find ways to engage legal changes without the same official pathways.

It is important to note that though many sites associated with sit-ins have been preserved in some way across the South; this is not the case in New Orleans. The Woolworth's building was demolished on February 23, 2015, and was slated to be replaced by a Hard Rock Hotel and condominium complex.[30] What was once McCrory's, the location of the second New Orleans sit-in that garnered national attention when the "CORE Four" took their case to the Supreme Court, was destroyed during Katrina and has since become a Ruby Slipper Cafe.[31] In a state where numerous plantation homes have been preserved as museums and bed-and-breakfast locations, I find it telling that two sites that led to major changes in civil rights have gone unprotected. Each of these examples makes clear the profound resistance to racial equality in the state of Louisiana as well as the variety of ways racism persists across time and space.

Five months after the 1960 Easter boycott organized by CLGNO, members of CORE staged the first lunch counter sit-in in the city.[32] Jerome Smith, Ruth Despenza, Joyce Taylor, William Harper, Archie Allen, and Tulane students Hugh Murray Jr. and William M. Harrell sat-in, were refused service, and were arrested. The group of protestors arrived at Woolworth's at 10:30 that morning and after being refused service, they explained they intended to stay. Local accounts indicate protestors smoked cigarettes and chatted with one another, as did the White patrons already seated at the counter who continued to receive service. Recall Augustine's emphasis on relationships that allow rhetors to choose when to seek to enlighten rather than seek to persuade. To the extent that the protestors engaged customers at the counter in everyday interactions and common practices, they emphasized that Black folks sitting at a lunch counter should not be unusual or unacceptable. Protestors did not offer a carefully structured and presented argument about why the counter should be integrated, instead they showed through their actions and interactions why other customers and restaurant owners should be comfortable with it. Sit-inners brought to the forefront the normalcy of sharing coffee and conversation regardless of the race of the customers. Consider too, that though six police officers were dispatched to Woolworth's, none of them acted in response to the protest until 12:30 when the lunch counter was shut down and the participants were arrested. This delay in response indicates the police officers stood by waiting to act, which allowed the protestors to stay at the lunch counter longer. The additional and unfettered time together increased the opportunity for locals to experience identification with the protestors, rather than focusing only on their differences.

After their arrests, other protestors marched in front of Woolworth's and carried signs that read, "Woolworth's Customers Jailed. We Walk for Their Freedom."[33] Accounts of this sit-in indicate it was uneventful. No violence. No heckling. None of the things characteristic of so many of the sit-ins that had preceded and then followed this one. The next week the McCrory Four were arrested for sitting in just down the street. Like the Woolworth's sit-in, the McCrory sit-in proceeded without the turmoil experienced in other locations. These initial sit-ins and marches were not enough to create the needed change. Instead, they were followed by numerous other acts of nonviolent social protest that lasted for many months. In fact, it took almost two years from the Woolworth's sit-in for the lunch counters in New Orleans to finally be integrated.

Photos in a series of articles published by *The Times Picayune* contribute to the narrative of the Woolworth's sit-in and help us gain more insight into what makes this sit-in unique.[34] In each of the photos there are relaxed bodies, relaxed faces, calm protestors, and representatives of the state. New Orleanians looked on as observers of the sit-in, some more concerned than others, but none of them jeering or attacking the protestors. This was not the story told in most civil rights protests; dogs, hoses, and violent attacks are much more common stories. And, while it all seems quite uneventful, that in and of itself becomes meaningful. As we saw sit-ins turn violent in many places, the New Orleans sit-in is painted in such a way as to indicate a complete lack of tumult. But according to the Veterans of the Civil Rights Movement, "crowds of angry whites taunt[ed], abuse[ed], and attack[ed] the CORE and NAACP demonstrators, beating them, scalding them with hot coffee, and throwing acid on them."[35] The discrepancies between the accounts is important. In an interview during the 50-year anniversary of the Canal Street sit-in, Rudy Lombard discussed having read about the Greensboro, NC, sit-ins and thinking, "That will never happen here. These people are too mean-spirited, too volatile."[36] Given all we know, it seems clear that the sit-ins in New Orleans were not as turmoil free as the images in the local paper might lead one to believe. The images tell what appears to be a sanitized version of what took place. They also situate Jerome Smith as a representative of the divine, an ordained intellectual engrossed in a *kairotic* moment.

Smith's participation in the civil rights movement did not start in 1960. When he was just ten years old, he watched his father remove a screen used to separate Black and White passengers on New Orleans' streetcars. The next week, while riding alone, he did the same. When White passengers became hostile, an older Black woman hit him and removed him from the streetcar apologizing to the White passengers. Once she safely escorted him out of view she cried, hugged him, and told him never to stop fighting for integration. Smith identifies this moment as the one that changed his life.[37] This represents a good example of Trapani and Maldonado's notion of *kairos* as metistic rhetoric. In these transformative moments, the young Smith acquired knowledge about integration and his role in bringing it to fruition. They made possible his choice to act reflexively then and later as an adult. His initial understandings and interactions led to a commitment rooted in dynamic and inventive actions. As an adult Smith became an integral part of CORE, participated in Freedom Rides, and founded Tambourine and Fan at the Treme Community Center, which is an after-school and summer program designed to cultivate social awareness among children in the neighborhood through music.[38]

Smith's work, as well as the work of his CORE colleagues, reveals a long trajectory of activism, all geared toward redefining an era. And, even though religious affiliation has generally been in decline in most U.S. states, 84% of Louisiana's residents still identified as Christian in 2019.[39] This makes clear the Christian ideology and iconography apparent in the Woolworth's sit-in are important in helping us understand how they functioned rhetorically. Additionally, Smith (and his colleagues) represented CORE at the sit-in, and CORE was developed by a preacher's son who had himself graduated from divinity school. This history led sit-inners to adopt practices of nonviolence they understood as an essential ideology of Christianity, as well as the direct actions associated with civil rights. A verse well-known by Christians and non-Christians alike is "But I am saying to you, you shall not rise up against an evil person, but whoever strikes you on your right cheek, turn to him also the other."[40] Because Smith and the other sit-inners were trained to withstand attacks without retaliation, "turning the other cheek" was an essential component to successfully sitting in. Also of importance is the notion that a person who does what is right according to the law of God will have God's blessings. More specifically, Christians are told "[. . .] whatever is true, whatever is honorable, whatever is right, whatever is pure, whatever is lovely, whatever is of good repute, if there is any excellence and if anything worthy of praise, dwell on these things. The things you have learned and received and heard and seen in me, practice these things, and the God of peace will be with you."[41] Sit-inners faced dangerous situations with this teaching as their backdrop. It became the idea that one can find peace in the face of violence and respond with what is honorable and right.

With these things in mind, I read Jerome Smith as the embodiment of a Christian rhetor whose mission was to aid in the integration of New Orleans. I turn now to three key pictures, taken by photographer Richard Uribe, who worked for the local newspaper, in which this characterization becomes clear. Here I note the importance of avoiding the inclination to psychologize the photographer and the editors of the *Times-Picayune*. The agency of the photographer and the editor is significant because they made choices—choices about how to frame the photos taken and which of the photos to print—but the way I read these images is only possible as a result of noticing various aspects of the photos that draw on recognizable Christian symbolism in relation to the sit-in and the history that accompanies it. It is the culmination of Smith's posture, his identification as a Christian, the choices of the photographer and editor, the specific location and time, and being part of a larger movement that lends itself to this understanding.

In the first image Smith is sitting at the counter reading a book, while New Orleans police officer Trosclair[42] talks with Joyce Taylor. Smith's hand is close to the page as if he is using it to guide his eye. His mouth is open as if he is reading aloud softly to himself. Smith seems unconcerned, almost unaware, of the police officer collecting information from Taylor. Because we know CORE members were trained in nonviolent strategies that drew on philosophy and religion, seeing a protestor in the process of studying highlights the intellectual aspects of this form of activism as well as a reliance on faith. The quiet disposition is also consistent with intellectualism and provides us with the image of an ideal protestor. Further, given the central importance of ethos, logos, and pathos in rhetorical practices, this photo implores the audience to see Smith as being reliable and of good character (ethos), situated in reasoned understandings (logos), and appealing to the humanity of onlookers (pathos). Placed in the context of Christian doctrine, the following verse allows us to read this image as a commitment to the wisdom of God. It reads, "I was with you in weakness and in fear and in much trembling, and my message and my preaching were not in persuasive words of wisdom, but in demonstration of the Spirit and of power, so that your faith would not rest on the wisdom of men, but on the power of God."[43] By focusing on Smith as a student, an intellectual who spends his time reading during the sit-in rather than talking with other sit-inners (or simply sitting) as his counterparts did, this photo introduces the idea of Smith as unique. It positions him as a thinker, and because of what we know about the training and foundations of the sit-in movement, as one who would likely draw on religious teachings to reinforce his fortitude in this difficult situation.

In a second photo Smith sits with his hands folded on the counter, as if in prayer. It is important to note that there is a white light that glows all around his head. This image calls forth notions of the Christian iconography associated with a halo. If read in this way, the halo is indicative of divine inspiration and support. Smith's mouth is slightly opened and pursed to one side. The picture is taken from a lower position than where Smith sits so that the angle is turned in a slightly upward direction and the viewer's eye is directed toward the sky. The perspective of size is also interesting. The picture creates a tunnel effect that causes Smith to look larger than life. Simultaneously, because the items on the counter are out of focus and appear to be the same size as Smith and the chairs closest to the camera lens seem particularly large, Smith appears small. As the eye gazes further back in the image, however, the people behind Smith appear even smaller than him. From what appears to be a good distance away, we can see Harrell's face, which is in tighter focus than Smith's face. It appears as if a line has been drawn to delineate Smith's back, neck, and face from the rest of the image. Furthermore, Smith's description that, "The civil rights movement was like church for me [. . .] It was about making things better" emphasizes that his involvement in and relationship to the civil rights movement grew out of a philosophical–religious perspective devoted to changing the world.[44] This image emphasizes the righteousness of the fight and invites the audience to think differently about the protest and integration. Rather than an explicit argument about the morally correct stance of extending rights to people of color, the Christian symbolism advanced an implicit appeal: what Augustine's theology would characterize as enlightenment and Burke would recognize as consubstantiation. Onlookers were given the opportunity to unconsciously connect their religious ideologies of love, grace, and acceptance with a political and social situation, and with people they had only seen themselves as separate from, to come to a new understanding.

In a third image Smith is being arrested for "criminal mischief" and escorted to the police wagon with a book under his arm and a rosary in his hand.[45] The cross that is hanging down from the rosary is highlighted by the dark suit of the man standing between Smith and Harrell. Because his shirt is blowing back behind him, one leg is bent indicating his step, and the beads are curving in toward his body; it is clear that Smith is in motion. Though the police officer's hand is blurry from movement, Smith is in perfect focus, as is the cross hanging from his hand. He presents no resistance, and the police appear calm as one of the officers keeps a hand on Smith's side. Because of the proximity of the book to the rosary, the book is more readily interpreted as a bible, and Smith as the "humble servant" working for the betterment of humankind becomes a reasonable way to interpret the image. This is consistent with the numerous religious leaders we see across the history of the movement, and the bible and prayer beads do much to trope that image. The prominence of his set jaw clarifies the emotional uproar and reinforces the significance of the event and this moment in time. As a civil rights activist, Smith becomes archetypal. Through the way he is represented in these photographs, this sit-in becomes a dynamic, righteous, and intellectual event. Again, Smith is positioned to enlighten the audience rather than persuade them. His actions, demeanor, and the symbolism around him present the message of integration and the extension of rights as coming from divine revelation. Thinking from the perspective of Augustine's conception of Christian rhetoric, this protest was designed to be used for the good of the people. It encouraged those who were unable to see the importance of integration to pay attention, and it helped those who had failed to understand before begin to grasp its significance.

As discussed earlier, the image-based narrative in the local newspaper positioned the residents of New Orleans as having reacted in a passive, non-aggressive way. This is inconsistent with residents of other cities across the South, as well as the personal accounts of the sit-inners.[46] It also fails to account for the two-year-long battle fought in New Orleans compared with the five months of protest that took place in Greensboro, NC, the place often heralded as a cornerstone of the sit-in movement.[47] Consider also the strength of the reaction four years after this sit-in took place among many White residents to the passing of the 1964 Civil Rights Act. John Pope wrote in a retrospective piece about integration in New Orleans that

> Opposition was fierce, as the files of letters to U.S. Rep. Hale Boggs, D-New Orleans, show. The Louisiana State Bar Association's House of Delegates, the organization's policy-making body, sent Boggs a copy of its resolution

denouncing the bill as a "violation of the rights to liberty, property and due process of law." An editorial in *The State Times*, Baton Rouge's afternoon newspaper, said it would "thrust deeply into the private lives of Americans everywhere." An anonymous writer said the bill was "clearly a tyrannical attempt to restore monarchy or establish dictatorship," while another writer warned Boggs, "Don't forget the white people elected you." A flier from E. M. Ruiz proclaimed, "Segregation is the law of God."[48]

These reactions indicate the images captured by the newspaper told a strategic version of this sit-in and the process of integration in the city of New Orleans. Did the photographer choose not to document the resistance and violence? Perhaps there are pictures that tell a different story, but the paper editor chose not to publish them. Or maybe the backlash experienced by the sit-inners who participated in this protest did not take place until later. Regardless of how it came to be, constructing the narrative in this way met the needs of the White audience. It allows politeness culture, the "bless her heart" approach to conflict, to persist in the face of highly charged political and social contestation. By en- couraging the perspective that the sit-ins were not going to disrupt the norms of the community, individuals who were resistant to the idea of integration could carry on as though it would all fade into the background. It also makes clear the unique nature of the local context and the kinds of rhetorical messages that could reach the audience. The sit-ins, the practice of sitting at a lunch counter, had become what Bekker refers to as a nonlocal strategy, something that is a congealed and repeatable structure, but the local context of New Orleans had immediate exigencies unique to the community that required a local response. In the face of the legal gymnastics performed by business owners and city and state government officials, New Orleans sit-inners had to respond by drawing on practical wisdom (*phronesis*) to educate the citizens (*paideia*).

The local White audience was only one of the audiences addressed by the images printed. The photos that position Jerome Smith as divinely appointed and the sit-ins as divinely inspired also serve to narrate the importance of individual participants and the sit-in strategy within the larger context of the civil rights movement in a nonlocal context. When students began using sit-ins as a strategy of rhetorical protest, they met resistance from established leaders in the civil rights movement, not just those opposed to integration. Recog- nized movement leaders were worried the student-led sit-ins would undo the progress that had been made up to that point. Brian Jones explained that the sit-ins organized by CORE in 1947 in Northern and Midwestern cities caused the NAACP to warn young members that "[a] disobedience movement on the part of Negroes and their White allies, if employed in the South, would result in wholesale slaughter with no good achieved."[49] In the face of concerns from the established members of the civil rights movement, laws, policies, practices, and hegemonic ideologies that subjugated Black people across the country, the photos became a powerfully persuasive tool for the students who stood not only in opposition to racial discrimination and separation but also to their elders in the civil rights movement. Given the philosophical foundations of the movement and the prevalence of religious ideologies, the idea that these strategies and the people implementing them were acting on behalf of a higher power resonated in profound ways and demonstrated the power of orthopraxis in the face of traditional orthodoxy.

As Rudy Lombard, one of the leaders of CORE said, the members in the New Orleans chapter were "courageous to the bone," and had "a certain confidence because they came out of a culture that was so rich: they knew that everything that was unique in the city could be traced to the Black presence."[50] Bolstered by the idea "that if the violence were only on the part of the White community, the world would see the *righteousness* of their cause" protestors were able to withstand attacks of all kinds and persist toward integration.[51] Thus, sit-inners' inventiveness effectively revealed the rhetorical power of Christian rhetoric, which was made apparent through Christian symbolism. The images represent a moment when, to draw on Bekker's notion of *kairos*, the prophetic spirit broke through the barriers of the law. The strategies, understanding of a changing situation, and ability to interrogate and transform all came together to create a powerful rhetorical appeal. Sit-ins as a rhetorical strategy of the civil rights movement developed from the lived experiences, philosophical and religious understandings, and commitment to change protestors knew was essential to the future of the country.

Conclusion

The exploration of the relationship among location, time, culture, and the participants in an event introduces distinctive possibilities of understanding. In this case, we gain insight into the ways the first lunch counter sit-in in New Orleans created an opportunity for change by relating to community members in a way that drew on local values, traditions, and customs. By reading the photos through the lens of Christian rhetoric and *Kairos*, it becomes clear that New Orleanian sit-inners moved beyond the traditional claim that it is fair and just to have integration. In this case, the call for integration appears divinely ordained. Rather than deliver carefully structured and powerfully delivered speeches like those given by Dr. Martin Luther King Jr. or Medgar Evers, sit-inners made it thinkable for White locals to change customs and practices once movement members were seen embodying the ethos of the divine. The Christian symbolism in the sit-inners' actions and their portrayal in photographs created a connection for resistant locals between their established values and beliefs and the push for integration. The notion of orthopraxis, the decision to act in response to social injustice even when it falls outside accepted orthodoxy, helps explain how young members were able to successfully question the older generation and their strategies. Thus, through identification with Christian symbols, the practices of sit-inners generally and Jerome Smith in particular, movement members educated the citizenry about the possibility for change. Smith and his cohort's actions redefined an era, a key characteristic of *kairos*, and asked members of the community at large, regardless of faith tradition, to stop and think about the implications of segregation. The history, traditions, demographics, laws, and prevalence of religion in New Orleans created a unique situation that demanded a unique response from movement members. By approaching these images from the perspective of Christian rhetoric and *kairos*, it becomes clearer why the Woolworth's sit-in opened the door for additional protests and the eventual integration of lunch counters across Louisiana. Sit-ins are also part of a long tradition of activism aimed at improving the lives of people of color through legal and social change. The effort to recognize, explore, and share events such as sit-ins become part of a course of change that began long before the 1960 New Orleans lunch counter sit-in and continues today.

Notes

1. Though this was the first sit-in to take place at a lunch counter in the city, civil rights activism has a long tradition in New Orleans. See Nikki Brown, "Jim Crow & Segregation," and John Bardes, "The New Orleans Streetcar Protests of 1867" for additional background.

2. John F. Kennedy, "Civil Rights Address."

3. "The Black Church, the Civil Rights Movement, and the Future," 95.

4. "Black Southern Student Sit-In Movement," 745.

5. For more information about personal experiences with sitting in see Moody, "Coming of Age in Mississippi," 31–33. For more on the personal choices behind participation in sit-ins see Searles and Williams, "Negro College Students' Participation in Sit-Ins," 215–20. For more regarding the outcome of various strategies see Wehr, "Nonviolence and Differentiation in the Equal Rights Movement," 65–76.

6. I have seen the word *kairos* written in numerous ways in various publications. In this essay, other than in the title, I have chosen to italicize rather than leave it unmarked or use a capital "k." In places where I use a direct quotation from an author who writes it differently, I write it as they do.

7. The second sophistic is a term used to describe the time period between 60 and 230 CE in which a Greek cultural movement emphasized the value and importance of public speaking, particularly speeches of declamation that were delivered with considerable emotion and that demonstrated the power of effective delivery strategies.

8. Kennedy, *Classical Rhetoric and Its Christian and Secular Tradition from Ancient to Modern Times*, 16–17.

9. Sutherland, "Augustine, Ethos and the Integrative Nature of Christian Rhetoric," 2.

10. Bizzell and Herzberg, 382.

11. Ibid., 382, 388.

12. Ibid., 11.

13. Ibid., 13.

14. Ibid., 17.

15. Kinneavy and Eskin, 434. Also, see William C. Trapani and Chandra A. Maldanado's essay, "Kairos: On the Limits to Our (Rhetorical) Situation" for a thorough discussion of how the understanding and application of *kairos* has changed over time.

16. Trapani and Maldanado, 281.

17. Ibid., 282–283.

18. Ibid., 283.

19. "Kairos and Carnival: Mikhail Bakhtin's Rhetorical and Ethical Christian Vision," 2.

20. Ibid., 3.

21. Ibid., 6.

22. Ibid., 4.

23. Wehr, "Nonviolence and Differentiation," 65.

24. Marcum, "Canal Street as a Venue of Social Change."

25. Hartford, "The Sit-Ins of 1960," 10.

26. Ibid.

27. The syllabus of the case reads: The court held that their conviction in this case was a violation of the Equal Protection Clause of the Fourteenth Amendment. The court explained that "Petitioners, three Negro students and one white student, entered a store in New Orleans, La., sat at a lunch counter reserved for white people, and requested service, which was refused. For refusing to leave when requested to do so by the manager of the store, they were convicted of violating the Louisiana Criminal Mischief Statute, which makes it a crime to refuse to leave a place of business after being ordered to do so by the person in charge of the premises. No state statute or city ordinance required racial segregation in restaurants, but both the Mayor and the Superintendent of Police had announced publicly that such 'sit-in demonstrations' would not be permitted." See *Lombard v. Louisiana*, 373 U.S. 267 (1963).

28. Reckdahl, "Sit-Ins at Canal Street Lunch Counters."

29. See *Lombard v. Louisiana*, 373 U.S. 267 as well as Reckdahl for further discussion of this case.

30. See Grunfeld, "Woolworth's Store in New Orleans is Demolished," and Thompson, "Plans Unveiled for Hard Rock Hotel, New Orleans."

31. The McCrory sit-in took place on September 16, 1960, just four days after New Orleans Mayor Chep Morrison issued a ban on sit-ins. Reckdahl, "Sit-Ins at Canal Street Lunch Counters." Pontchartrain, "Did New Orleans Have any Sit-Ins?"

32. On March 28, 1960, seven Southern University students sat-in at Kress Five and Dime in downtown Baton Rouge. The next day, nine Southern University students sat-in at Sitman's Drugstore and the Greyhound Bus Station. Both days all sit-inners were arrested for disturbing the peace. See "Baton Rouge Students Sit-In for U.S. Civil Rights (Southern University 16), 1960" for more about these sit-ins.

33. See Reckdahl, "Sit-In at McCrory's."

34. All images originally available in an online (now defunct) archive (http://photos .nola.com/tag/civil%20rights/photos-oldest.html) were maintained by *The Times Picayune* ("Gallery: Lunch Counter Demonstration in the 60s"). Although the photo of Smith being arrested is no longer available online, the other two images included in this essay

can be found at https://www.nola.com/news/politics/article_b39cddf6-1ae6-586e-a5c4-897 d9fa9ad06.html.

35. "New Orleans Merchant Boycotts & Sit-ins (1960–1963)."

36. Reckdahl, "Sit-Ins at Canal Street Lunch Counters."

37. "I Put the Screen Down, Took a Seat, and the Streetcar Became Hostile."

38. His ongoing contribution to the community was made clear when, on May 3, 2012, Gilbert Crowden began a petition to change the name of the Treme Community Center to Jerome Smith Treme Community Center. See "Treme Community Center Name Change!" for more about Smith, his work in the community, and his relationship with the center. See also the 2017 video posted by the Treme Center titled, "Jerome Smith, Unsung Hero," available at https://vimeo.com/212698168.

39. "Louisiana Population 2020."

40. Matthew 5:39 (New King James Version [NKJV]).

41. Philippians 4:8–9 (NKJV).

42. I was unable to find a record of officer Trosclair's first name.

43. 1. Corinthians 2:3–5 (NKJV).

44. Ibid.

45. "New Orleans Merchant Boycotts & Sit-ins (1960–1963)." In an interview with third graders at Martin Luther King Charter School in New Orleans in 2011, Smith discussed this specific moment. He told them, "An Italian lady came up to me and gave me her prayer beads. The police told her not to, but she wouldn't leave. She gave me her prayer beads, and she told me I was right." See Stroup, "6th Graders Hear about Civil Rights" for the full interview. This gesture and statement from the local woman creates an explicit link to Smith's action as being consistent with Christian principles and made clear that he had support from at least one woman who was willing to let her position be known in front of the police enforcing local custom.

46. For example, Hugh Murray moved out of his parents' house after they received bomb threats. Oretha Castle lost her job at Hotel Dieu hospital. Lanny Goldfinch was hung in effigy at Tulane and couldn't get life insurance because of all the death threats. See Reckdahl, "Sit-Ins at Canal Street Lunch Counters."

47. In this book we have made a concerted effort to correct an inaccurate understanding that the sit-in that took place in Greensboro started the sit-in movement. Even so, most popular press and scholarly treatments of the sit-ins perpetuate this idea. See Reckdahl's "Sit-Ins at Canal Street Lunch Counters" for more on the timeline to integration in New Orleans.

48. Pope, "Civil Rights Act Started Changing America, and New Orleans, a Half-century Ago."

49. Jones, "The Sit-ins that Ignited the Movement."

50. See Reckdahl, "Sit-in at McCrory's."

51. "The Sit-In Movement" (emphasis added).

AFTERWORD

The Embers that Remain

Sean Patrick O'Rourke & Lesli K. Pace

In this collection we've considered five sit-ins that took place in 1960. These were not the only sit-ins that took place that year, but they provide examples of the rhetorical power and significance of sit-ins as part of the civil rights movement. Across the decade there were numerous sit-ins, wade-ins, and demonstrations. These demonstrations also reinvigorated members of the movement and garnered attention from media and government officials, propelling the discussion further into the national zeitgeist. By August 1963 members of the movement were able to organize one of the largest demonstrations of the era, the "March on Washington," which was the site of Martin Luther King Jr.'s widely known "I Have a Dream" speech.[1] Within a few short weeks of the march, one of the deadliest acts of violence committed against participants in the movement occurred when the Sixteenth Street Baptist Church in Birmingham, Alabama, was bombed during the congregation's Youth Day celebration.[2]

As 1963 came to an end, Congress, with the Civil Rights Act of 1964, used its Commerce Clause power to guarantee "full and equal" access to and enjoyment of "any place of public accommodation . . . without discrimination or segregation on the ground of race, color, religion, or national origin."[3] The act swept away the last feeble attempts to justify segregation in public accommodations on a private-property theory and opened a new era of legal protection for citizens who, only four years before, had been routinely denied service in, and sometimes even access to, most stores, inns, libraries, restaurants, beaches, skating rinks, and countless other places. We have learned, however, that such hard-won gains are all too often followed by reaction, backlash, and retrenchment.

As Congress debated and voted upon this legislation, civil rights activists continued working to make changes. But, in the wake of the civil rights movement's early successes came the well-publicized murders of James Chaney,

Andrew Goodman, and Mickey Schwerner at the start of Mississippi Freedom Summer.[4] The period also saw the assassinations of Malcolm X and Martin Luther King Jr. in 1965 and 1968, massive White flight in the late 1960s and 1970s, and the long resistance to busing and affirmative action in the 1970s and 1980s.[5]

While these events were disjointed, uncoordinated, and of course not directly responsive to the sit-in protests, they were quite clearly opposed to the underlying principles—integration, racial equality, and equal accommodation—of the movement. They have been followed by repeated attempts to undercut both the Civil Rights Act of 1964 and the Voting Rights Act of 1965, undermine and roll back important legal and constitutional advances made under the Warren Court—including a slow erosion of *Brown v. Board of Education*—and move the nation steadily away from the rapid and progressive change of the early 1960s.[6] The pattern of advancement and reaction on matters of race is as present now as it has ever been. Talk of a "post-racial America" with the election of President Barack Obama in 2008 proved premature and has been followed by battles over neo-Confederate monuments, rebel battle flags, police violence against people of color, voter ID laws and intimidation, and a surge of race-based backlash that supported the candidacy and unlikely presidency of Donald Trump.

What, then, are the legacies of the civil rights era sit-ins? We find the story they tell is one of contrasting words and images, contested public memories, fragmented but enduring lessons, and an ongoing effort to find justice. The sit-ins are still present but in far more complicated ways than we may have imagined. Take for example the role of documentary style programing in helping current generations learn about this part of U.S. history, the role of museums that stage moments from the civil rights movement, or the memorials and historical markers designed to recognize the 1960 wade-ins on the beaches of Biloxi, Mississippi, that turned so violent that the day became known as "Bloody Sunday."[7] In each of these cases the narratives constructed make clear that efforts to remember also entail a powerful form of forgetting.[8]

But what of the influences of civil rights protest strategies on more contemporary movements? The occupation of Alcatraz Island by the Indians of All Tribes from November 1969 until June 1971 is one example of a protest that resembles the sit-ins of the civil rights movement.[9] Often thought of as the beginning of the "Red Movement," this occupation drew national attention to the mistreatment and poor living conditions of Native Americans by reclaiming space that had once been theirs. The "Chicano Moratorium" in August 1970 also shares commonalities with the demonstrations of the civil rights movement such as the youth demonstrations in Alabama. What began as a peaceful protest at Laguna Park in Los Angeles in response to the disproportionate number of Mexican Americans dying in the Vietnam War ended in violence and the death of four protestors.[10]

During the 1980s protests in the United States ranged from an international anti-nuclear armament rally to a one-person sit-in in response to the development of the National Civil Rights Museum.[11] Movements of the 1990s focused on disability rights, racial equality, access to reproductive services, and environmental protection.[12] Whether through the specific strategies employed, or because of the intersecting issues addressed in the protest, activism across the decades share important similarities worthy of rhetorical investigation.

In the first two decades of the 2000s, social media have become an integral part of activism. Though sometimes dismissed as the armchair quarterback of activism, in recent years the impact of social media on activism has grown exponentially. From aiding activists in staging protests against their government —as in the Arab Spring—to serving as a vehicle for victims of sexual assault and race-based police brutality to assert their voices and find support—as in the Me Too and Black Lives Matter movements—technology has allowed activists to develop new ways to share information and new methods of organizing.

Still, as we have worked to complete this book in the summer of 2020 we have been struck not only by the parallels between the 1960 sit-ins and today's protests but also by the several ways that thinking about sit-ins deepens and enriches our understanding of a new age of public dissent. The central thrust of sit-in protests—bodies occupying contested spaces to highlight inequities or injustices—is evident in a wide range of twenty-first century activism. From marriage-equality advocates occupying public buildings where officials refused to recognize same-sex marital rights and teachers striking outside of public schools to highlight cuts in education funding to the Dakota Pipeline Protests at Standing Rock and the "police-free" area known as the Capitol Hill Autonomous Zone created by allies of Black Lives Matter in Seattle, protesters deployed a corporal or somatic rhetoric by putting their bodies in contested places. Like the lunch counters and libraries and swimming pools of the sit-in movement, those places became sites of protest, locations of rhetorical influence.[13] And this rhetoric is evident now not only in left-leaning or progressive protests but also in campaigns and demonstrations from the right and far-right. Consider the Bundy brothers' and members of the sovereign citizens movement's armed occupation of the Malheur National Wildlife Refuge headquarters in 2016 or Michigan United for Liberty's armed stand-ins at the Michigan Capitol to protest Governor Gretchen Witmer's COVID-19 "stay at home" orders or even unmasked so-called "civil rights" activists occupying "masks required" places during the same coronavirus crisis.[14] Each of these recent protests is a form of sit-in or stand-in that echoes, with considerable variations in tone, those of sixty years before.

Thinking through recent protests in light of the analyses offered in this book can enrich and complicate our understanding of them. For example, Richard Leeman's analysis of the Charlotte and Rock Hill sit-ins helps us understand how different communities can cultivate and express very different responses to protests that are, in most important ways, quite similar, as well as how violence can engulf one community and not another. Similarly, Lesli Pace's essay enables us to understand the importance of visual argument so that when we see, for example, "Taking a Stand in Baton Rouge," Jonathan Bachman's already "legendary" photograph of Leshia Evans at a Black Lives Matter protest, we can more fully appreciate the transformative power of a single image.[15] Sean O'Rourke's and Stephen Schneider's essays remind us that protests are rarely monolithic or singular occurrences and that the multifaceted dimensions of protest are best understood by observing how they unfold over time and in response to the changing conditions of their local and regional contexts. And the lines of thought that run through the essays—the trope of "outside agitators," for instance, or the charge of "socialism," or Christianity as a lens that both distorts and magnifies—are still with us today.

By exploring the similarities and connections across events in a single movement or between different movements, we have an opportunity to understand the nature and function of both.[16] The challenge, then, for scholars and students of rhetoric is to continue exploring the strategies that are deployed, to look for interesting connections among and between protests and protests strategies, and to argue how answering these questions enhances our understanding of the power of rhetoric.[17]

Notes

1. While King's speech is the one most widely known from this event, A. Philip Randolph, Roy Wilkins, John Lewis, and other movement members spoke before King. For more information see the "March on Washington" entry in the *Civil Rights Digital Library*.

2. "Birmingham Bombing (Sixteenth Street Baptist Church)."

3. Civil Rights Act of 1964; Commerce Clause. U.S. Const. art. I, § 8, cl. 3.

4. See, e.g., Huie, *Three Lives for Mississippi*; Ball, *Murder in Mississippi*; Cagin and Dray, *We Are Not Afraid*; Watson, *Freedom Summer*; and McAdam, *Freedom Summer*.

5. For a good sense of what these two assassinations meant and continue to mean for America, see Cone, *Martin and Malcolm and America*. For an interesting study of White flight in one southern city, see Kruse, *White Flight*. Two important studies on busing include Delmont, *Why Busing Failed* and Formisano, *Boston against Busing*.

6. On attempts to gut the Civil Rights Act, see the rather sweeping discussion at the Gates Public Service Law Program titled, "The Rollback of Civil Rights Era in America." For the Voting Rights Act, see Rutenberg, "A Dream Undone." On the erosion of *Brown*, see, in particular, *Parents Involved in Community Schools v. Seattle School District No. I*, 551

U.S. 701 (2007). But see also Wilkinson, "The Seattle and Louisville School Cases" (arguing that the court decided the cases correctly).

7. On documentary studies of the sit-ins, see, e.g., DeLaure, "Televisuality and the Performance of Citizenship on NBC's 'Sit-In.'" On civil rights museums, see Bowen, "Visualizing a Civil Rights Archive: Images of the Sit-In at the Counter and Other Objects." For a study of civil rights memorials and historical markers, see Funderburk and Atkins-Sayre, "Forgetting the 1960 Biloxi, Mississippi Wade-Ins."

8. Funderburk and Atkins-Sayre, e.g., demonstrate that Mississippi's attempt to construct the Mississippi Freedom Trail commemorating important state sites and events in civil rights history "are motivated by the belief that forgetting a painful past removes barriers to healing" and that reconciliation requires "that the conversation is halted, the haunting details omitted, and memory sanitized." They conclude that "Rembrance, no matter how painful, may be necessary to unmaks the evils of the past truly" but concede that "motivations to forget seem far more likely" (275).

9. For more on this occupation, listen to "Radio Free Alcatraz."

10. To learn more about this protest, listen to "Chicano Moratorium."

11. For more on this protest see Montgomery, "Throngs Fill Manhattan to Protest Nuclear Weapons." For a deeper understanding of the one-person sit-in in Memphis, see Worthington, "The Longest Sit-In."

12. For more information on the march and sit-in focusing on rights for those with disabilities, see "1990—Atlanta—Cassie James." For information regarding the long-term implications of the "Battle of Seattle" protest, see Scruggs, "What the Battle of Seattle Means 20 Years Later."

13. On marriage equality protests, the prominent case of Kentucky county clerk Kim Davis's refusal to issue marriage licenses to same-sex couples even after the U.S. Supreme Court's marriage equality decision in *Obergefell v. Hodges* (576 U.S. 644, 2015) overshadowed many protests of such refusals. See, e.g., the protests in the small town of Dothan, AL, in "Equality Wiregrass Plans to Protest." On teachers, see Yan, "Here's What Teachers Accomplished" and Wolf, "Why Teacher Strikes are Touching." On the pipeline protests, see Levin, "Dakota Access Pipeline." And on Seattle's Capitol Hill, see Kiley et al., "Seattle Police Clear CHOP Protest Zone."

14. On the Malheur sit-in see Wolf, et al., "Armed Men," and Anti-Defamation League, "Anatomy of a Standoff." On the Michigan protests see Censky, "Heavily Armed Protesters." For the masking order defiance, see, e.g., Armentrout, "Front-Line Face-Offs."

15. "Baton Rouge Killing: Black Lives Matter Protest Photo Hailed as 'Legendary.'" *BBC News*, July 11, 2016, https://www.bbc.com/news/world-us-canada-36759711.

16. Del Gandio, "Direct Action Then and Now: Comparing the Sit-Ins and Occupy Wall Street."

17. For some direction, see Miller, "Afterword: Chiseling at a Fossilized Memory."

Selected Bibliography

"Airport 'March' Peaceful," *Greenville (SC) Piedmont,* January 2, 1960.

"Airport Protest is Held," *Greenville (SC) Piedmont,* January 1, 1960.

"Aldermen 'Kill' Human Relations Bill," *Louisville (KY) Defender,* April 28, 1960.

Andrews, Kenneth T., and Michael Biggs. "The Dynamics of Protest Diffusion: Movement Organizations, Social Networks, and News Media in the 1960 Sit-Ins." *American Sociological Review* 71 (2006): 752–77.

Anti-Defamation League. "Anatomy of a Standoff: The Occupiers of the Malheur National Wildlife Refuge Headquarters." 2015. https://www.adl.org/sites/default/files/documents/assets/pdf/combating-hate/Anatomy-of-a-Standoff-MalheurOccupiers.pdf.

Armentrout, Mitchell. "Front-Line Face-Offs: Mask Rule Sparks Threats, Rebellion, Shouting at Store Workers: 'And We Can't Do Anything about It,'" *Chicago Sun-Times,* May 5, 2020, https://chicago.suntimes.com/politics/2020/5/5/21248762/illinois-grocery-store-mask-requirement-coronavirus-retailers.

Bainbridge, Judith. "Integrating Greenville's Library in 1960," *Greenville (SC) News,* July 14, 2016, https://www.greenvilleonline.com/story/life/2016/07/14/integrating-greenvilles-library/87084922/.

Ballenger, William L. "City Library Calm During 'Sitdown,'" *Greenville (SC) Piedmont,* March 17, 1960.

———. "Negroes Stage Sit-Ins at City Lunch Counters," *Greenville (SC) Piedmont,* July 18, 1960.

———. "Violence Flares on Main Street: Officers Break Up Incident," *Greenville (SC) Piedmont,* July 21, 1960.

Ball, Howard. *Murder in Mississippi: United States v. Price and the Struggle for Civil Rights.* Lawrence: University Press of Kansas, 2004.

"Baptists Against Negro Protests," *Charlotte (NC) Observer,* February 27, 1960.

Bardes, John. "The New Orleans Streetcar Protests of 1867." *We're History,* http://werehistory.org/the-new-orleans-streetcar-protests-of-1867/.

Bartley, Numan V. *The New South: 1945–1980.* Baton Rouge: Louisiana State University Press, 1995.

"Baton Rouge Students Sit-In for U.S. Civil Rights (Southern University 16), 1960." *Global Nonviolent Action Database: U.S. Civil Rights Movement (1950s-1960s).* Accessed February 1, 2020, https://nvdatabase.swarthmore.edu/content/baton-rouge-students-sit-us-civil-rights-southern-university-16-1960.

Battles, David M. *The History of Public Library Access for African Americans in the South: Or, Leaving Behind the Plow.* Lanham, MD: Scarecrow Press, 2009.

Bayor, Ronald H. "Atlanta, Georgia, 1960–1961: Sit-Ins and Student Activism." *Georgia Historical Quarterly* 75 (1991): 557–65.

Bekker, Ian. "Kairos and Carnival: Mikhail Bakhtin's Rhetorical and Ethical Christian Vision." *Religions* 79 (2018): 1–11.

Bell, Derrick. *Silent Covenants: Brown v. Board of Education and the Unfulfilled Hopes for Racial Reform.* New York: Oxford University Press, 2006.

Benford, Robert. "An Insider's Critique of the Social Movement Framing Perspective." *Sociological Inquiry* 67 (1997): 409–30.

Benford, Robert, and David Snow. "Framing Processes and Social Movements: An Overview and Assessment." *Annual Review of Sociology* 26 (2000): 611–39.

"A Better Strategy," *Louisville (KY) Defender,* January 28, 1960.

Bilbo, Theodore B. *Take Your Choice: Separation or Mongrelization.* Poplarville, MS: Dream House Publishing, 1947.

"Birmingham Bombing (Sixteenth Street Baptist Church)." *Civil Rights Digital Library,* http://crdl.usg.edu/cgi/crdl?action=retrieve;rset=001;recno=2.

Bizzell, Patricia, and Bruce Herzberg. *The Rhetorical Tradition: Readings from Classical Times to the Present.* 2nd ed. Boston: Bedford/St. Martin's, 2001.

Black, Edwin. "Gettysburg and Silence." *Quarterly Journal of Speech* 80 (1994): 21–36.

"Bowling Segregation Is Cause of Disagreement," *Louisville (KY) Defender,* October 6, 1960.

Brady, Tom P. *Black Monday.* Winona, MS: Association of Citizens' Councils, 1955.

"Brother 'Rock' Earned His Welcome," *Charlotte (NC) Observer,* March 2, 1960.

Brown, Nikki. "Jim Crow & Segregation." *64 Parishes.* https://64parishes.org/entry/jim-crow segregation.

"Brown Theater Protest Points Up Bias Problem," *Louisville (KY) Defender,* January 14, 1960.

Burke, Kenneth. *Language as Symbolic Action: Essays of Life, Literature, and Method.* Berkeley: University of California Press, 1966.

———. *A Rhetoric of Motives.* Berkeley: University of California Press, 1969.

Bynum, Thomas L. *NAACP Youth and the Fight for Black Freedom, 1936–1965.* Knoxville: University of Tennessee Press, 2013.

Cagin, Seth, and Philip Dray. *We Are Not Afraid: The Story of Goodman, Schwerner, and the Civil Rights Campaign for Mississippi.* New York: Macmillan, 1988.

Caldwell, Paul. "Citizen's Council Leader Urges Law, Not Violence," *Rock Hill (SC) Herald,* February 17, 1960.

"Can't Eat—Don't Buy," *Louisville (KY) Defender,* June 2, 1960.

Carson, Clayborne. *In Struggle: SNCC and the Black Awakening of the 1960s.* Cambridge, MA: Harvard University Press, 1981.

Cartwright, Samuel. "Report on the Diseases and Physical Peculiarities of the Negro Race." Originally in the *New Orleans Medical and Surgical Journal* (1851) and *DeBow's Review* (1851). Available at https://www.pbs.org/wgbh/aia/part4/4h3106t.html.

Cassie, Ron. "And Service for All: Sixty Years Ago, Morgan State College Students Staged the First Successful Lunch-Counter Sit-Ins," *Baltimore Magazine,* January 19, 2015, http://www.baltimoremagazine.com/2015/1/19/morgan-students-staged-reads-drugstore-sit-in-60-years-ago.

Censky, Abigail. "Heavily Armed Protesters Gather Again at Michigan Capitol to Decry Stay-At-Home Order," *National Public Radio,* May 14, 2020, https://www.npr.org/2020/05/14/855918852/heavily-armed-protesters-gather-again-at-michigans-capitol-denouncing-home-order.

Chafe, William H. *Civilities and Civil Rights: Greensboro, North Carolina, and the Black Struggle for Freedom.* New York: Oxford University Press, 1981.

"Chapel Hill Scene of Negro Protests," *Charlotte (NC) Observer,* March 1, 1960.

"Charlotte People are Enlightened," *Charlotte (NC) Observer,* March 1, 1960.

"Charlotte People are Fair Minded," *Charlotte (NC) Observer,* March 1, 1960.

"Chicano Moratorium." *American Archive of Public Broadcasting.* https://americanarchive
.org/catalog/cpb-aacip_28-6t0gt5fp55.

"CIO Delegates 'Sit In' at Columbia Hotel as Waitresses Refuse to Serve Negroes." *New York Times,* March 17, 1947.

"CIO Group Stages Coffee Shop 'Sit-in' As Racial Protest," *Washington Post,* March 18, 1947.

"Citizens Rally to Hear CORE Leader," *Louisville (KY) Defender,* April 28, 1960.

Civil Rights Act of 1964, tit. II, §§ 201–207 (1964). (Current version at 42 U.S.C. § 2000a (2017)).

Claiborne, Jack. "41 Raleigh Negroes Arrested in Protest for Food Service," *Charlotte (NC) Observer,* February 13, 1960.

"Close Counter Rather Than Serve Negroes: Miami CORE Heads Fight on Race Bias." *Chicago Defender,* September 26, 1959.

Code of Greenville, 1953, as amended in 1958.

"Color Lines in North." *Charlotte (NC) Observer,* February 24, 1960.

Cone, James H. *Martin and Malcolm and America.* Maryknoll, NY: Orbis Books, 1990.

"A Conference is in Order Now." *Charlotte (NC) Observer,* February 20, 1960.

Conley, Thomas M. *Rhetoric in the European Tradition.* Chicago: University of Chicago Press, 1994.

"The Contrast Was Painful." *Rock Hill (SC) Herald,* March 3, 1960.

"Cool Heads Should Not Be Rushed." *Charlotte (NC) Observer,* March 1, 1960.

Covington, Roy. "Negroes Continue Protest at Diners." *Charlotte (NC) Observer,* February 11, 1960.

———. "Negroes' Protests Close Local Diners." *Charlotte (NC) Observer,* February 10, 1960.

———. "'Sitdown' Is Explained By Students." *Charlotte (NC) Observer,* February 12, 1960.

———. "Smith University Students Suspend Demonstrations." *Charlotte (NC) Observer,* February 19, 1960.

———. "Students Hope to Talk it Over." *Charlotte (NC) Observer,* February 12, 1960.

Crocker, James W. "Judge Dismisses Library Suit Here." *Greenville (SC) News,* September 15, 1960.

"A Crisis of Conscience." *Louisville (KY) Defender,* March 16, 1961.

"Curfew Keeps City Quiet; Officials Say No Plans to Lift It." *Greenville (SC) News,* July 29, 1960.

Davis, Virginia. "Meet Disappoints Citizens' Leaders." *Rock Hill (SC) Herald,* March 21, 1960.

———. "Rock Hill Negroes Threaten Boycott." *Rock Hill (SC) Herald,* March 1, 1960.

Day, John Kyle. *The Southern Manifesto: Massive Resistance and the Fight to Preserve Segregation.* Jackson: University Press of Mississippi, 2014.

"A Decision is Needed But Overdue." *Charlotte (NC) Observer,* February 29, 1960.

"The Decision of the Supreme Court in the School Cases: A Declaration of Constitutional Principles." [The "Southern Manifesto."] *Congressional Record,* 84th Congress, Second Session 102 (March 12, 1956) 4459–60.

DeLaney, Theodore Carter. "The Sit-In Demonstrations in Historic Perspective." *The North Carolina Historical Review* 87.4 (2010): 431–38.

Delmont, Matthew F. *Why Busing Failed: Race, Media, and the National Resistance to School Desegregation.* Berkeley: University of California Press, 2016.

"Democracy is a Two-Way Street," *Charlotte (NC) Observer,* March 5, 1960.

"Democracy Isn't For a Few People," *Charlotte (NC) Observer,* March 14, 1960.

"Demonstrations Reveal Symptoms," *Charlotte (NC) Observer,* March 5, 1960.

"The Demonstrators Are U.S. Citizens," *Charlotte (NC) Observer,* March 4, 1960.

Dionisopoulos, George N., Victoria J. Gallagher, Steven R. Goldzwig, and David Zarefsky. "Martin Luther King, The American Dream, and Vietnam: A Collision of Rhetorical Trajectories." *Western Journal of Communication* 56 (1992): 91–107.

"Divine's Followers Give Aid to Strikers: With Evangelist's Sanction They 'Sit Down' in Restaurant," *New York Times,* September 23, 1939.

"Does the South Have Peculiar Sadism?" *Charlotte (NC) Observer,* March 7, 1960.

Doster, Joe. "Negroes Protest City Police 'Manhandling,'" *Charlotte (NC) Observer,* March 1, 1960.

Driver, Justin. "Supremacies and the Southern Manifesto." *Texas Law Review* 92 (2014): 1053–135.

Eberhart, George M. "The Greenville Eight: The Sit-In that Integrated the Greenville (S.C.) Library." *American Libraries,* June 1, 2017, https://americanlibrariesmagazine.org /2017/06/01/greenville-eight-library-sit-in/.

Edgar, Walter B. *South Carolina: A History.* Columbia: University of South Carolina Press, 2011.

"An Editorial," *Louisville (KY) Defender,* January 7, 1960.

Egerton, John. *Speak Now Against the Day: The Generation before the Civil Rights Movement in South.* New York: Knopf, 1995.

Eick, Gretchen Cassel. *Dissent in Wichita: The Civil Rights Movement in the Midwest, 1954–1972.* Urbana: University of Illinois Press, 2001.

Endres, Danielle, and Samantha Senda-Cook. "Location Matters: The Rhetoric of Place in Protest." *Quarterly Journal of Speech* 97 (2011): 257–82.

"Equality Wiregrass Plans to Protest Probate Judge's Refusal to Issue Marriage Licenses," *Dothan (AL) Eagle,* July 10, 2015, https://www.dothaneagle.com/archives/equality wiregrass-plans-to-protest-probate-judges-refusal-to-issue-marriage-licenses/article_682 defae-271d-11e5-a2d7-eb30261137ec.html.

Equal Protection Clause. U.S. Const. amend. XIV, § 1.

"Evangelical Church Approves Sit Down," *Charlotte (NC) Observer,* February 21, 1960.

"Everybody Wants To Be Accepted," *Charlotte (NC) Observer,* March 18, 1960.

"Everyone Loses in the Sit Down," *Charlotte (NC) Observer,* February 7, 1960.

Fairclough, Adam. *Better Day Coming: Black and Equality, 1890–2000.* New York: Viking, 2001.

Farber, David, and Beth Bailey. *The Columbia Guide to America in the 1960s.* New York: Columbia University Press, 2001.

Fayer, Steve. "Ain't Scared of Your Jails." *Eyes on the Prize,* season 1, episode 3. Directed by Orlando Bagwell. Aired on PBS, February 4, 1987.

"Federal Intervention Necessary," *Louisville (KY) Defender,* June 2, 1955.

"Fighting Erupts During 'Protest,'" *Charlotte (NC) Observer,* February 16, 1960.

Fischer, Roger A. "A Pioneer Protest: The New Orleans Street-Car Controversy of 1867." *Journal of Negro History* 53 (1968): 219–33.

Fleming, Cynthia Griggs. "White Lunch Counters and Black Consciousness: The Story of the Knoxville Sit-Ins." *Tennessee Historical Quarterly* 49 (1991): 40–52.

Flono, Fannie. "Helping Charlotte Find Its Way—50 Years Ago," *Charlotte (NC) Observer,* May 30, 2013.

"Forcing One's Rights Can Be Disastrous," *Charlotte (NC) Observer,* March 10, 1960.

Formisano, Ronald P. *Boston Against Busing: Race, Class, and Ethnicity in the 1960s and 1970s.* Chapel Hill: University of North Carolina Press, 1991.

Fosl, Catherine, and Tracy K'Meyer. *Freedom on the Border: An Oral History of the Civil Rights Movement in Kentucky.* Lexington: University Press of Kentucky, 2010.

Franks, Dorothy, Ben Downs, and Sean Patrick O'Rourke. "Communicating Civic Responsibility & Reconciliation: A Keynote 'Conversation.'" Carolinas Communication Association, Greenville, SC, Friday, October 3, 2014.

Gadzekpo, Leonard. "The Black Church, the Civil Rights Movement, and the Future." *Journal of Religious Thought* 53/54 (1997): 95–112.

Gallagher, Victoria J., Kenneth S. Zagacki, and Jeffrey C. Swift. "From 'Dead Wrong' to Civil Rights History: The Durham Royal Seven, Martin Luther King's 1960 'Fill Up the Jails' Speech, and the Rhetoric of Visibility." In *Like Wildfire: The Rhetoric of the Civil Rights Sit-Ins,* edited by Sean Patrick O'Rourke and Lesli K. Pace, 80–101. Columbia: University of South Carolina Press, 2020.

Gamson, William. "Constructing Social Protest." In *Social Movements and Culture,* edited by Hank Johnston and Bert Klandermans, 85–106. Minneapolis: University of Minnesota Press, 1995.

Garrow, David J. *Atlanta, Georgia, 1960–1961: Sit-ins and Student Activism.* Brooklyn, NY: Carlson Pub, 1989.

Gilmore, Glenda Elizabeth. *Defying Dixie: The Radical Roots of Civil Rights, 1919–1950.* New York: Norton, 2008.

"God Isn't Color Blind," *Charlotte (NC) Observer,* February 24, 1960.

Goldfield, David. *Black, White, and Southern: Race Relations and Southern Culture, 1940 to the Present.* Baton Rouge: Louisiana State University Press, 1990.

"Good Will Stands at Lunch Counters," *Charlotte (NC) Observer,* February 26, 1960.

Goodrich, Peter. "Rhetoric and Somatics: Training the Body to do the Work of Law." *Law Text Culture* 5 (2000–01): article 9, https://ro.uow.edu.au/cgi/viewcontent.cgi?article =1063&context=ltc

Gordon, Linda. *The Second Coming of the KKK: The Ku Klux Klan of the 1920s and the American Political Tradition.* New York: W.W. Liveright, 2017.

Graham, Patterson Toby. *A Right to Read: Segregation and Civil Rights in Alabama's Public Libraries, 1900–1965.* Tuscaloosa: University of Alabama Press, 2002.

Gravely, William. "The Civil Right Not to Be Lynched: State Law, Government, and Citizenship Response to the Killing of Willie Earle (1947)." In *Toward the Meeting of the Waters,* edited by Winfred B. Moore and Orville Vernon Burton, 93–118. Columbia: University of South Carolina Press, 2008.

Graves, Carl R. "The Right to be Served: Oklahoma City's Lunch Counter Sit-Ins, 1958–1964." *Chronicles of Oklahoma* 59 (1981): 151–66.

"The Greenville Civil Rights Movement." Panel Discussion at the Greenville County Library, Greenville, SC, August 22, 2013.

Griffin, Leland M. "When Dreams Collide: Rhetorical Trajectories in the Assassination of President Kennedy." *Quarterly Journal of Speech* 70 (1984): 111–31.

"Groans from Dying Practices," *Louisville (KY) Defender,* January 17, 1957.

Grossman, Ron. "The Birth of the Sit-In," *Chicago Tribune,* February 23, 2014, http:// articles.chicagotribune.com/2014-02-23/news/ct-hyde-park-sit-in-0223-20140223_1_ezell -blair-lunch-counter-blacks.

Grunfeld, David. "Woolworth's Store in New Orleans is Demolished, Site of the 1960 First Locally Organized Lunch Counter Sit-in" *The Times-Picayune,* updated July 17, 2019, https://www.nola.com/news/politics/article_3994e989-69f4-5c18-9671-4f839 bf10f65.html.

"Gunfire Breaks Out as Races Clash in Greenville: Number of Arrests Are Made," *Greenville (SC) News,* July 26, 1960.

Halberstam, David. "A Good City Gone Ugly." *The Reporter,* March 31, 1960. 17–19. In *Reporting Civil Rights: Part One,* 440–46.

Hall, Jacqueline Dowd. "The Long Civil Rights Movement and the Political Uses of the Past." *Journal of American History* 91 (2005): 1233–63.

Harcourt, Felix. *Ku Klux Kulture: America and the Klan in the 1920s.* Chicago: University of Chicago Press, 2017.

Hart, T. Robert, Jr. "Amend or Defend: The End of Jim Crow in Greenville and Charleston." MA thesis, Clemson University, 1997.

Hartford, Bruce. "The Sit-Ins of 1960." *The Civil Rights Movement Archive.* Accessed October 1, 2011. http://www.crmvet.org/info/sitins.pdf.

Heffner, Earl. "Hundreds Arrested as Negroes Protest," *Charlotte (NC) Observer,* March 16, 1960.

"Hefner's Bible Not Like Hers," *Charlotte (NC) Observer,* March 14, 1960.

Hill, Jennifer E. M. "Reframing the Victim: Rhetoric for Segregation in the Greenville News." *Young Scholars in Writing: Undergraduate Research in Writing and Rhetoric* 9 (2011): 45–57.

Hine, William C. "The 1867 Charleston Streetcar Sit-Ins." *The South Carolina Historical Magazine* 77 (1976): 110–14.

"The History of CORE." *The Congress of Racial Equality.* Accessed October 1, 2011. http://www.core-online.org/Features/History/history.htm.

Hochschild, Adam. "Ku Klux Klambakes." *The New York Review of Books,* December 7, 2017, 16–18.

"Hollings Has No Comment On Report," *Rock Hill (SC) Herald,* February 26, 1960.

Hoover, Judith D. "The Nashville Sit-Ins: Successful Nonviolent Direct Action through Rhetorical Invention and Advocacy." In *Like Wildfire: The Rhetoric of the Civil Rights Sit-Ins,* edited by Sean Patrick O'Rourke and Lesli K. Pace, 102–23. Columbia: University of South Carolina Press, 2020.

"How Not to Attract," *Louisville (KY) Defender,* May 19, 1955.

Hudson, Janet G. *Entangled by White Supremacy: Reform in World War I Era South Carolina.* Lexington: University of Kentucky Press, 2008.

Huff, Archie Vernon, Jr. *Greenville: The History of the City and County in the South Carolina Piedmont.* Columbia: University of South Carolina Press, 1995.

Huie, William Bradford. *Three Lives for Mississippi.* New York: WCC Books, 1965.

Hurst, Rodney L. *It Was Never about a Hot Dog and a Coke!: A Personal Account of the 1960 Sit-In Demonstrations in Jacksonville, Florida and Ax-Handle Saturday.* Livermore, CA: WingSpan Press, 2008.

"I Put the Screen Down, Took a Seat, and the Streetcar Became Hostile." *Storycorps.* Accessed October 1, 2011. https://storycorps.org/stories/jerome-smith-and-carol-bebelle/.

Ingram, T. Robert, ed., *Essays on Segregation.* Houston, TX: St. Thomas Press, 1960.

"Integration is Matter of Mind," *Charlotte (NC) Observer,* March 6, 1960.

"Intolerance Shows One's Inferiority," *Charlotte (NC) Observer,* February 21, 1960.

"It Can Happen Here," *Louisville (KY) Defender,* March 10, 1960.

Johnson, Nan. *Gender and Rhetorical Space in American Life.* Carbondale: Southern Illinois University Press, 2002.

Jones, Bob, Sr. *Is Segregation Scriptural?* Greenville, SC: Bob Jones University, 1960.

Jones, Brian. "The Sit-ins that Ignited the Movement." *Socialist Worker.org,.* February 1, 2010, https://socialistworker.org/2010/02/01/sit-ins-that-ignited-a-movement.

Kelley, Blair L. M. *Right to Ride: Streetcar Boycotts and African American Citizenship in the Era of* Plessy v. Ferguson. Chapel Hill: University of North Carolina Press, 2010.

Kennedy, George A. *Classical Rhetoric and Its Christian and Secular Tradition from Ancient to Modern Times.* Chapel Hill: University of North Carolina Press, 1980.

Kennedy, John F. "Civil Rights Address." *American Rhetoric,* June 11, 1963, https://american rhetoric.com/speeches/jfkcivilrights.htm.

Kiley, Brendan, Ryan Blethen, Sydney Brownstone, and Daniel Beekman, "Seattle Police Clear CHOP Protest Zone," *Seattle Times,* July 2, 2020, https://www.seattletimes.com /seattle-news/seattle-police-clearing-chop-protest-zone/.

Kilpatrick, James Jackson. *The Southern Case for School Segregation.* n.p.: Crowell-Collier Press, 1962.

King, Martin Luther, Jr. "I've Been to the Mountaintop." 1968. Martin Luther King, Jr. Research and Education Center, Stanford University. http://kingencyclopedia.stanford .edu/encyclopedia/documentsentry/ive_been_to_the_mountaintop/.

Kinneavy, James L., and Catherine R. Eskin. "Kairos in Aristotle's Rhetoric." *Written Communication* 17 (2000): 432–45.

"Klan, White Youths Vie for Seats with Negro Students in Diner Protest," *Charlotte (NC) Observer,* February 6, 1960.

Kluver, Randolph. "Rhetorical Trajectories of Tiananmen Square." *Diplomatic History* 34 (2010): 71–94.

K'Meyer, Tracy. *Civil Rights in the Gateway to the South: Louisville, Kentucky, 1945–1980.* Lexington: University Press of Kentucky, 2010.

Knott, Cheryl. *Not Free, Not for All: Public Libraries in the Age of Jim Crow: The Untold History of Public Library Integration.* Amherst: University of Massachusetts Press, 2015.

Kruse, Kevin M. *White Flight: Atlanta and the Making of Modern Conservatism.* Princeton, NJ: Princeton University Press, 2005.

Landry, Stuart Omer. *The Cult of Equality: A Study of the Race Problem.* New Orleans, LA: Pelican Publishing, 1945.

Lau, Peter F. *Democracy Rising: South Carolina and the Fight for Black Equality Since 1865.* Lexington: University of Kentucky Press, 2006.

Lawrence, Noah. "Since It Is My Right, I Would Like to Have It: Edna Griffin and the Katz Drug Store Desegregation Movement." *The Annals of Iowa* 67 (2008): 298–330.

Lehn, Melody. "Liminal Protest: Eleanor Roosevelt's 'Sit-Between' at the 1938 Southern Conference for Human Welfare." In *Like Wildfire: The Rhetoric of the Civil Rights Sit-Ins,* edited by Sean Patrick O'Rourke and Lesli K. Pace, 19–37. Columbia: University of South Carolina Press, 2020.

"Let's Seek Lunch Counter Peace," *Charlotte (NC) Observer,* March 8, 1960.

Levin, Sam. "Dakota Access Pipeline: The Who, What, and Why of the Standing Rock Protests." *The Guardian,* November 3, 2016, https://www.theguardian.com/us-news/2016 /nov/03/north-dakota-access-oil-pipeline-protests-explainer.

Lewis, Andrew B. *The Shadows of Youth: The Remarkable Journey of the Civil Rights Generation.* New York: Hill & Wang, 2009.

Lewis, Camille Kaminski. "A is for Archive: The Politics of Research in the Southern Archive." *Carolinas Communication Annual* 31 (2015): 15–18.

Lewis, George. *Massive Resistance: The White Response to the Civil Rights Movement.* London: Oxford University Press, 2006.

———. "'Complicated Hospitality': The Impact of the Sit-Ins on the Ideology of Southern Segregationists." In *From Sit-Ins to SNCC: The Student Civil Rights Movement in the*

1960s, edited by Iwan Morgan and Philip Davies, 41–57. Gainesville: University Press of Florida, 2012.

Long, Michael G., ed. *First Class Citizenship: The Civil Rights Letters of Jackie Robinson.* New York: Time Books of Henry Holt, 2007.

"Louisiana." *History.* Accessed November 1, 2019. https://www.history.com/topics/us-states /louisiana.

"Louisiana Population 2020 (Demographics, Maps, Graphs)," http://worldpopulation review.com/states/louisiana-population/.

"Louisville Public Places Present Dismal Picture of Discrimination," *Louisville (KY) Defender,* November 29, 1956.

"The Lunch Counter Dollar is 'Different,'" *Charlotte (NC) Observer,* March 1, 1960.

"Lunch Counter Sitdown Resumes in Rock Hill," *Rock Hill (SC) Herald,* February 23, 1960.

"Lunch Issue No Public Affair," *Charlotte (NC) Observer,* February 15, 1960.

"Lunchroom Counters Still Segregated Here," *Louisville (KY) Defender,* January 19, 1956.

"March on Washington," *Civil Rights Digital Library,* http://crdl.usg.edu/events/march_on _washington/?Welcome.

Marcum, Anna. "Canal Street as a Venue of Social Change During the Civil Rights Movement." *Preservation in Print,* September 18, 2019, https://prcno.org/canal-street-venue -social-change-civil-rights-movement/.

McAdam, Doug. *Freedom Summer.* New York: Oxford University Press, 1988.

McElwee, Sean, and Jason McDaniel. "Economic Anxiety Didn't Make People Vote Trump, Racism Did." *The Nation,* May 8, 2017, https://www.thenation.com/article/economic -anxiety-didnt-make-people-vote-trump-racism-did/.

McNeill, William. *Keeping Together in Time: Dance and Drill in Human History.* Cambridge, MA: Harvard University Press, 1995.

Meier, August. *Negro Thought in America, 1880–1915: Racial Ideologies in the Age of Booker T. Washington.* Ann Arbor: University of Michigan Press, 1963.

Meier, August, and Elliott Rudwick. "Negro Boycotts of Segregated Streetcars in Virginia, 1904–1907." *The Virginia Magazine of History and Biography* 81 (1973): 479–87.

Mendelson, Michael. *Many Sides: A Protagorean Approach to the Theory, Practice, and Pedagogy of Argument.* Dordrecht, The Netherlands: Kluwer Academic Publishers, 2002.

Middleton, Michael, Aaron Hess, Danielle Endres, and Samantha Senda-Cook. *Participatory Critical Rhetoric: Theoretical and Methodological Foundations for Studying Rhetoric In Situ.* Lanham, MD: Lexington Books, 2015.

"Militancy Is the Watchword," *Louisville (KY) Defender,* November 22, 1956.

"Ministers: Racial Fight Must End," *Charlotte (NC) Observer,* March 16, 1960.

"Mississippi Injustice," *Louisville (KY) Defender,* September 15, 1955.

Mixon, Harold. "The Rhetoric of States' Rights and White Supremacy." In *A New Diversity in Contemporary Southern Rhetoric,* edited by Calvin M. Logue and Howard Dorgan, 166–87. Baton Rouge: Louisiana State University Press, 1987.

Mohl, Raymond A. "Interracial Activism and the Civil Rights Movement in Postwar Miami." *Tequesta* 66 (2006): 28–48.

———. "'South of the South': Jews, Blacks, and the Civil Rights Movement in Miami, 1945–1960." *Journal of American Ethnic History* 18 (1999): 3–36.

Molina, David Miguel. "'Our Boys, Our Bonds, Our Brothers': Pauli Murray and the Washington, DC, Sit-Ins, 1943–1944." In *Like Wildfire: The Rhetoric of the Civil Rights Sit-Ins,* edited by Sean Patrick O'Rourke and Lesli K. Pace, 38–59. Columbia: University of South Carolina Press, 2020.

Montgomery, Paul. "Throngs Fill Manhattan to Protest Nuclear Weapons," *New York Times,* June 13, 1982.

Moody, Anne. "Coming of Age in Mississippi." *Literary Cavalcade* 537 (2001): 31–33.

Moore, Winfred B., Jr., and Orville Vernon Burton, eds. *Toward the Meeting of the Waters: Currents in the Civil Rights Movement of South Carolina During the Twentieth Century.* Columbia: University of South Carolina Press, 2008.

"Moral Integrity and Lunch Counters," *Charlotte (NC) Observer,* February 22, 1960.

Morgan, Iwan W. "The New Movement: The Student Sit-Ins in 1960." In *From Sit-Ins to SNCC: The Student Civil Rights Movement in the 1960s,* edited by Iwan Morgan and Philip Davies, 1–22. Gainesville: University Press of Florida, 2012.

Morgan, Iwan W., and Philip Davies, eds. *From Sit-Ins to SNCC: The Student Civil Rights Movement in the 1960s.* Gainesville: University Press of Florida, 2012.

Morris, Aldon. "Black Southern Student Sit-In Movement: An Analysis of Internal Organization." *American Sociological Review* 46 (1981): 744–67.

Morton, Samuel. *Crania Americana, or, A Comparative View of the Skulls of Various Aboriginal Nations of North and South America: To Which is Prefixed an Essay on the Varieties of the Human Species.* Philadelphia: J. Dobson, 1839.

Mountford, Roxanne. "On Gender and Rhetorical Space." *Rhetoric Society Quarterly* 31 (2001): 41–71.

Munn, Porter. "Negro Demonstrators Wave Money and Signs," *Charlotte (NC) Observer,* February 28, 1960.

"NAACP Pickets Brown Theater," *Louisville (KY) Defender,* December 31, 1959.

"Negro Boycott Wouldn't Hurt Merchants," *Rock Hill (SC) Herald,* March 7, 1960.

"Negro Group Backed," *Charlotte (NC) Observer,* February 5, 1960.

"The Negro Needs Answers for Questions," *Rock Hill (SC) Herald,* March 12, 1960.

"Negro Press Creed," *Louisville (KY) Defender,* March 18, 1952.

"The Negro Press Is You," *Louisville (KY) Defender,* March 18, 1952.

"Negro Youth Invade RH Lunch Counters," *Rock Hill (SC) Herald,* February 12, 1960.

"Negroes Are Right," *Charlotte (NC) Observer,* February 19, 1960.

"Negroes Conduct Orderly Segregation Protest Here: About 250 March on Airport," *Greenville (SC) News,* January 2, 1960.

"Negroes Seek Diner Service," *Charlotte (NC) Observer,* February 3, 1960.

"Negroes to Stay Til Served," *Charlotte (NC) Observer,* February 4, 1960.

"New Orleans Merchant Boycotts & Sit-ins (1960–1963)." *Veterans of the Civil Rights Movement–Timeline.* Accessed March 1, 2011. http://www.crmvet.org/tim/timhis60.htm #1960nosmb.

"New Sit-Down Staged Here; Curfew Violator is Fined: Negroes Take Seats at 2 Variety Stores," *Greenville (SC) News,* July 30, 1960.

"9 pm Curfew Ordered to Ease Racial Unrest, No County Action At This Time: Persons 20 Years or Younger to Be Affected," *Greenville (SC) News,* July 27, 1960.

"1990—Atlanta—Cassie James." *ADAPT—Free Our People!* https://adapt.org/1990-atlanta -cassie-james/.

"No Trouble Here Unless . . . ," *Life,* September 17, 1956, 109–10.

Noakes, John, and Hank Johnston. "Frames of Protest: A Road Map to a Perspective." In *Frames of Protest: Social Movements and the Framing Perspective,* edited by Hank Johnston and John Noakes, 1–29. Lanham, MD: Rowman and Littlefield, 2005.

Norris, Marjorie M. "An Early Instance of Non-Violence: The Louisville Demonstrations, 1870–71." *Journal of Southern History* 32 (1966): 487–504.

"A Notable Anniversary," *Louisville (KY) Defender,* May 12, 1955.

Oberdorfer, Don. "Charlottean's Debates Stun Red Hunters," *Charlotte (NC) Observer,* February 6, 1960.

———. "Negroes Expect Integrated Cafeteria," *Charlotte (NC) Observer,* March 8, 1960.

O'Brien, M. J. *We Shall Not Be Moved: The Jackson, Woolworth's Sit-In and the Movement It Inspired.* Jackson: University Press of Mississippi, 2013.

Olds, Victoria M. "Sit-Ins: Social Action to End Segregation." *Social Work* April (1961): 99–105.

Olson, Lynne. *Freedom's Daughters: The Unsung Heroines of the Civil Rights Movement from 183–1970.* New York: Scribner, 2001.

O'Neill, Stephen. "Memory, History, and the Desegregation of Greenville, South Carolina." In *Toward the Meeting of the Waters,* edited by Winfred B. Moore Jr. and Orville Vernon Burton, 286–99. Columbia: University of South Carolina Press, 2008.

Oppenheimer, Martin. *The Sit-In Movement of 1960.* Brooklyn, NY: Carlson Pub, 1989.

"Ordinance Needed to End 'Accommodations' Bias," *Louisville (KY) Defender,* December 4, 1958.

O'Rourke, Sean Patrick. "Circulation and Noncirculation of Photographic Texts in the Civil Rights Movement: A Case Study in the Rhetoric of Control." *Rhetoric and Public Affairs* 15 (2012): 685–94.

———. "Greenville Airport Protest Started an Avalanche," *Greenville (SC) News,* January 2, 2010.

———. "Racism's Lessons Learned in Upstate: A 60-Year Retrospective," *Greenville (SC) News,* June 14, 2007.

O'Rourke, Sean Patrick, and Lesli K. Pace, eds. *Like Wildfire: The Rhetoric of the Civil Rights Sit-Ins.* Columbia: University of South Carolina Press, 2020.

Ortlepp, Anke. *Jim Crow Terminals: The Desegregation of American Airports.* Athens: University of Georgia Press, 2017.

"Other Folks Say: Some Racial Facts and Fallacies," *Rock Hill (SC) Herald,* March 28, 1960.

"Our Anniversary," *Louisville (KY) Defender,* April 2, 1952.

"Parents Unanimously Approve Curfew But Teen-Agers Somewhat Reluctant," *Greenville (SC) News,* July 17, 1960.

Perelman, Chaïm, and Lucie Olbrechts-Tyteca. *The New Rhetoric: A Treatise on Argumentation.* Translated by John Wilkinson and Purcell Weaver. Notre Dame, IN: University of Notre Dame Press, 1969.

Peterson v. Greenville, oral arguments at *Peterson v. City of Greenville,* Oyez, https://www.oyez.org/cases/1962/71.

Phillips, Kendall R. "A Rhetoric of Controversy." *Western Journal of Communication* 63 (1999): 488–510.

"Pilgrimage by Negroes Set Today," *Greenville (SC) News,* January 1, 1960.

Pontchartrain, Blake. "Did New Orleans Have any Sit-ins During the Civil Rights Era?" *The Advocate,* April 15, 2019, https://www.theadvocate.com/gambit/new_orleans/news/blake_pontchartrain/article_ecd123a0-5afb-11e9-b391-a77f6942cd8b.html.

Pope, John. "Civil Rights Act Started Changing America, and New Orleans, a Half-Century Ago," *The Times-Picayune,* June 27, 2014, https://www.nola.com/news/politics/article_6f717f2d-1e5b-5684-9afb-f740e247585b.html.

"Pride or Principle in Lunch Question?" *Charlotte (NC) Observer,* February 24, 1960.

"Protests Possess Gandhian Character," *Charlotte (NC) Observer,* February 27, 1960.

Proudfoot, Merrill. *Diary of a Sit-In.* Chapel Hill: University of North Carolina Press, 1962.

"Public Accommodations Bias Protest Begins," *Louisville (KY) Defender,* January 22, 1959.

Quigley, Joan. "How D.C. Ended Segregation a Year before *Brown v. Board of Education*," *Washington Post,* January 15, 2016, https://www.washingtonpost.com/opinions/the -forgotten-fight-to-end-segregation-in-dc/2016/01/15/1b7cae2a-bafc-11e5-829c-26ffb874 a18d_story.html?utm_term=.8b8df3dce049.

"Radio Free Alcatraz." *American Archive of Public Broadcasting.* https://americanarchive .org/catalog/cpb-aacip_28-5717m0482m.

Ray, Angela G. "The Transcript of a Continuing Conversation: David Zarefsky and Public Address." *Argumentation and Advocacy* 45 (2008): 64–79.

Reckdahl, Katy. "Sit-Ins at Canal Street Lunch Counters 50 Years Ago Sparked a Civil Rights Case that Went All the Way to the Supreme Court," *The Times-Picayune,* September 17, 2010, https://www.nola.com/news/politics/article_159ae236-6e76-53d9-b1dc -d4ac2fb6c335.html.

———. "Sit-in at McCrory's: September 17, 1960." *New Orleans Historical,* https://new orleanshistorical.org/items/show/1399.

Regnault, John F. "Indictment of Christopher Jones in the Richmond City Hustings Court." *Remaking Virginia: Transformation Through Emancipation,* http://www.virginiamemory .com/online-exhibitions/items/show/587.

Reporting Civil Rights: Part One, America Journalism, 1941–1963. Library of America 137. New York: Literary Classics, 2003.

Ritchie, Gladys. "The Sit-In: A Rhetoric of Human Action." *Today's Speech* 18 (1970): 22–25.

"Robeson Affair Quite Different," *Charlotte (NC) Observer,* March 2, 1960.

Robinson-Simpson, Leola Clement. *Greenville County South Carolina.* Black America Series. Charleston, SC: Arcadia Publishing, 2007.

"The Rollback of Civil Rights Era in America," *Gates Public Service Law Program,* January 25, 2008, https://www.law.washington.edu/multimedia/2008/rollback/transcript.pdf.

Rutenberg, Jim. "A Dream Undone: Inside the 50-year Campaign to Roll Back the Voting Rights Act," *New York Times Magazine,* July 29, 2015, https://www.nytimes.com/2015 /07/29/magazine/voting-rights-act-dream-undone.html?mcubz=1.

Salisbury, Harrison E. "Fear and Hatred Grip Birmingham," *New York Times,* April 12, 1960, In *Reporting Civil Rights: Part One,* 447–52.

"S.C. Bill Would Halt 'Sit-Down' Movement," *Charlotte (NC) Observer,* February 18, 1960.

"S.C. Bills Would Nip Sit-Downs," *Charlotte (NC) Observer,* March 3, 1960.

Schmidt, Christopher W. *The Sit-Ins: Protest & Legal Change in the Civil Rights Era.* Chicago: University of Chicago Press, 2018.

"Schools Shouldn't Encourage Youths," *Charlotte (NC) Observer,* February 21, 1960.

Scott, Robert L., and Donald K. Smith. "Rhetoric of Confrontation." *Quarterly Journal of Speech* 55 (1969): 1–8.

Scruggs, Gregory. "What the 'Battle of Seattle' Means 20 Years Later." *City Lab,* https:// www.citylab.com/life/2019/11/seattle-wto-world-trade-organization-protest-riot-1999/60 2806/.

Seals, Donald, Jr., "The Wiley-Bishop Student Movement: A Case Study in the 1960 Civil Rights Sit-Ins." *Southwestern Historical Quarterly* 106 (2003): 418–40.

Searles, Ruth, and J. Allen Williams Jr. "Negro College Students' Participation in Sit-Ins." *Social Forces* 40.3 (1962): 215–20.

"Sentiment Can't Solve the Problem," *Charlotte (NC) Observer,* March 6, 1960.

"'Separate But Equal' Plan Upheld," *Charlotte (NC) Observer* (Regional edition), March 15, 1960.

Shaheen, Fred. "Citizens Council Unit Planned at Rock Hill," *Charlotte (NC) Observer,* February 17, 1960.

———. "Food Counter Protest Canceled by Weather," *Charlotte (NC) Observer,* February 14, 1960.

———. "Law Can Stop Negro Protests, Senator Says," *Charlotte (NC) Observer,* February 26, 1960.

———. "Mayor Asks Policy on Lunch Counters," *Charlotte (NC) Observer,* February 26, 1960.

———. "Negroes Resume Rock Hill Protest," *Charlotte (NC) Observer,* February 24, 1960.

"Sit-Downs Prove Negroes Not Satisfied with Being of an Inferior Status," *Louisville (KY) Defender,* March 31, 1960.

"Sit-In Leader Advises Appeal to Moral Issues," *Louisville (KY) Defender,* May 5, 1960.

"Sit-In Leader Lawson at NAACP Meet Here," *Louisville (KY) Defender,* April 28, 1960.

"The Sit-In Movement," *U.S. History Online Textbook,* accessed November 1, 2019, http://www.ushistory.org/us/54d.asp.

"Sit-Ins, a Weapon of Choice?" *Louisville (KY) Defender,* August 11, 1960.

Sitton, Claude. "Negro Sitdowns Stir Fear of Wider Unrest in the South," *New York Times,* February 15, 1960. In *Reporting Civil Rights: Part One,* 433–40.

Sloane, Thomas O. *On the Contrary: The Protocol of Traditional Rhetoric.* Washington, DC: The Catholic University of America Press, 1999.

"Smith Alumni Backing Students," *Charlotte (NC) Observer,* February 23, 1960.

Snook, Harry. "Four Rock Hill Stores Are Hit by Protest," *Charlotte (NC) Observer,* February 13, 1960.

Snow, David, and Robert Benford. "Master Frames and Cycles of Protest." In *Frontiers in Social Movement Theory,* edited by Aldon Morris and Carol McClurg, 133–55. New Haven, CT: Yale University Press, 1992.

Snow, David, E., Burke Rochford Jr., Steven K. Worden, and Robert D. Benford. "Frame Alignment Processes, Micromobilization, and Movement Participation." *American Sociological Review* 51 (1986): 464–81.

"The Socialists Push Integration," *Charlotte (NC) Observer,* March 1, 1960.

"Some Questions in Race Relations," *Charlotte (NC) Observer,* February 22, 1960.

Southern Regional Council. "Special Report: Student Protest Movement, Winter, 1960." Southern Regional Council Papers, 1944–68. Ann Arbor, MI: University Microfilms, 1984.

Stanley, Frank. "Being Frank about People, Places, and Problems," *Louisville (KY) Defender,* August 18, 1951.

———. "Being Frank about People, Places, and Problems," *Louisville (KY) Defender,* April 2, 1952.

———. "Being Frank about People, Places, and Problems," *Louisville (KY) Defender,* January 6, 1955.

———. "Being Frank about People, Places, and Problems," *Louisville (KY) Defender,* September 15, 1955.

———. "Being Frank about People, Places, and Problems," *Louisville (KY) Defender,* February 9, 1956.

———. "Being Frank about People, Places, and Problems," *Louisville (KY) Defender,* March 15, 1956.

———. "Being Frank about People, Places, and Problems," *Louisville (KY) Defender,* November 29, 1956.

———. "Being Frank about People, Places, and Problems," *Louisville (KY) Defender,* December 6, 1956.

———. "Being Frank about People, Places, and Problems," *Louisville (KY) Defender,* August 20, 1959.

———. "Being Frank about People, Places, and Problems," *Louisville (KY) Defender,* April 21, 1960.

———. "Being Frank about People, Places, and Problems," *Louisville (KY) Defender,* September 22, 1960.

———. "Being Frank about People, Places, and Problems," *Louisville (KY) Defender,* March 9, 1961.

"State License Is Not 'Private,'" *Charlotte (NC) Observer,* March 10, 1960.

Stokes, J. Hunter. "7 Negroes Walk into Library Here," *Greenville (SC) News,* March 17, 1960.

———. "14 Young Negroes Are Arrested After Sit-In," *Greenville (SC) News,* August 10, 1960.

"Stores Are Not Restaurants," *Charlotte (NC) Observer,* February 17, 1960.

Stroup, Sheila. "6th Graders Hear about Civil Rights Struggles Right from Local Leader's Mouths." *NOLA.com* March 27, 2011. www.nola.com/books/index.ssf/2011/03/6th_graders_hear_about_civil_r.html.

"Student 'Sit-Ins' Emerge as a Vital Force to Be Reckoned With," *Louisville (KY) Defender,* January 3, 1960.

"Student 'Sit-Ins' Is Top Controversy in United States," *Louisville (KY) Defender,* March 24, 1960.

"Students Cause Trouble," *Charlotte (NC) Observer,* February 20, 1960.

"Students Continuing Lunch Counter Drive," *Charlotte (NC) Observer,* February 18, 1960.

"Students Form Non-violence Coordination Group at Raleigh Conference of Eight-State Leaders," *Louisville (KY) Defender,* April 21, 1960.

"Students Pursue Goals at Home," *Charlotte (NC) Observer,* March 12, 1960.

"Students Seek Aid of Negro Adults," *Charlotte (NC) Observer,* March 14, 1960.

"Students' Viewpoint in Protest," *Charlotte (NC) Observer,* February 21, 1960.

"Students Win Sit-In Victory in N.C. Court," *Louisville (KY) Defender,* April 28, 1960.

Sullivan, Patricia. "Lawyer Samuel Tucker and His Historic 1939 Sit-In at Segregated Alexandria Library," *Washington Post,* August 7, 2014, https://www.washingtonpost.com/local/lawyer-samuel-tucker-and-his-historic-1939-sit-in-at-segregated-alexandria-library/2014/08/05/c9c1d38e-1be8-11e4-ae54-0cfe1f974f8a_story.html?utm_term=.1e4256ac1448.

Sutherland, Christine Mason. "Augustine, Ethos, and the Integrative Nature of Christian Rhetoric." *Rhetor: Journal of the Canadian Society for the Study of Rhetoric* 1 (2004): 1–18.

Suyuan, Sun. "Collective Identity and International Politics: A Cultural Perspective." In *Cultural Factors in International Relations,* edited by Xintian Yu, 67–78. Washington, DC: The Council for Research in Values and Philosophy, 2004.

Terrill, Robert E. "Rhetorical Criticism and Citizenship Education." In *Purpose, Practice, and Pedagogy in Rhetorical Criticism,* edited by Jim A. Kuypers, 163–76. Lanham, MD: Lexington Books, 2014.

"They Protest Arrest of Demonstrators," *Rock Hill (SC) Herald,* March 19, 1960.

"Thinks Everyone Should Be Served," *Charlotte (NC) Observer,* March 17, 1960.

Thompson, James W. "Whites, Negroes in Street Battle: Clash Follows Sit-Ins Here," *Greenville (SC) News,* July 22, 1960.

Thompson, Richard. "Plans Unveiled for Hard Rock Hotel, New Orleans: 18 floors, 350 rooms on Canal Street," *The New Orleans Advocate,* February 15, 2018, https://www.nola.com/news/business/article_782b5dbc-9d2a-59e2-96a5-9b6048df5007.html.

Timms, Leslie. "3 Counter Sit-Ins Held in Greenville," *Greenville (SC) News,* July 19, 1960.

———. "8 Negroes Sit-In at Library Here: Arrested and Jailed Briefly," *Greenville (SC) News,* July 17, 1960.

Trapani, William C., and Chandra A. Maldonado. "Kairos: On the Limits to Our (Rhetorical) Situation." *Rhetoric Society Quarterly* 48 (2018): 278–86.

"Treme Community Center Name Change!" https://sign.moveon.org/petitions/treme-community-center.

Tucker, Ray. "Negroes' Sitdowns Stir New Discord," *Greenville (SC) News*, March 22, 1960.

Turner, Kathleen J., ed. *Doing Rhetorical History: Concepts and Cases.* Tuscaloosa: University of Alabama Press, 1998.

"Two Negroes Eat at White Church Here," *Charlotte (NC) Observer,* March 17, 1960.

"Understanding Leads to Race Harmony," *Charlotte (NC) Observer,* March 4, 1960.

Varda, Scott J. "Sit-In as Argument and the Perils of Misuse." *Argumentation and Advocacy* 55 (2019): 132–51.

Walker, Anders. "Legislating Virtue: How Segregationists Disguised Racial Discrimination as Moral Reform Following *Brown v. Board of Education.*" *Duke Law Journal* 47 (1998): 399–424.

Walker, Devona. "50 Years Ago, Children Helped Change Nation When They Sat Down." *The Oklahoman*, August 19, 2008, http://newsok.com/article/3285497.

Walker, Ruth. "Group of Young Negroes Enters Greenville Library: Building is Close by Trustees," *Greenville (SC) News*, March 2, 1960.

———. "Integration Local Library Is Sought: Negroes File Federal Suit," *Greenville (SC) News*, July 29, 1960.

Washburn, Mark. "Hawkins' Way—and Charlotte's—Helped Restaurants Integrate," *Charlotte (NC) Observer,* May 25, 2013.

Watson, Bruce. *Freedom Summer: The Savage Season of 1964 That Made Mississippi Burn and Made America a Democracy.* New York: Viking Press, 2010.

"Wave of Protest Gets Legion Action," *Louisville (KY) Defender*, October 15, 1959.

Webb, Clive, ed. *Massive Resistance: Southern Opposition to the Second Reconstruction.* Oxford: Oxford UP, 2005.

Wehr, Paul E. "Nonviolence and Differentiation in the Equal Rights Movement." *Sociological Inquiry* 38 (1968): 65–76.

"A Welcome Voice of Restraint," *Rock Hill (SC) Herald,* February 18, 1960.

West, Rebecca. "Opera in Greenville," *The New Yorker*, June 14, 1947, https://www.newyorker.com/magazine/1947/06/14/opera-in-greenville.

"What a Record? Louisville Leads Nation in Sit-In Arrests," *Louisville (KY) Defender*, April 27, 1961.

"White and Negro Teen-Agers Clash: At Local Drive-In," *Greenville (SC) News*, July 25, 1960.

White, James Boyd. *When Words Lose Their Meaning: Constitutions and Reconstitutions of Language, Character, and Community.* Chicago: University of Chicago Press, 1984.

"White and Negro Teen-Agers Clash: At Local Drive-In," *Greenville (SC) News*, July 25, 1960.

"Whites, Negroes Scuffle in Some Areas," *Charlotte (NC) Observer,* February 25, 1960.

"Why Don't the Silent Speak?" *Rock Hill (SC) Herald,* March 24, 1960.

Wickenberg, Charles. "Hollings Hits Ike's Race Talk," *Charlotte (NC) Observer,* March 17, 1960.

Wiegand, Wayne A., and Shirley A. Wiegand. *The Desegregation of Public Libraries in the Jim Crow South: Civil Rights and Local Activism.* Baton Rouge: Louisiana State University Press, 2018.

Wilder, Rip. "600 Hear Gressette Push Citizens Council," *Rock Hill (SC) Herald,* February 26, 1960.

———. "Two Rock Hill Lunch Counters Close; Seats Removed,' Drug Stores Re-Open," *Rock Hill (SC) Herald,* February 13, 1960.

Wilkerson, Isabell. *The Warmth of Other Suns: The Epic Story of America's Great Migration.* New York: Random House, 2010.

Wilkinson, J. Harvie, III. "The Seattle and Louisville School Cases: There Is No Other Way." *Harvard Law Review* 121 (2007): 158–83.

William Gravely Oral History Collection on the Lynching of Willie Earle. South Caroliniana Library of the University of South Carolina University Libraries. http://digital.tcl.sc.edu/cdm/landingpage/collection/gravely.

Williams, Jessica. "Rudy Lombard, New Orleans Civil Rights Activist and Author, Dies at 75," *The Times-Picayune,* December 14, 2014, https://www.nola.com/news/politics/article_170962e1-a073-5f52-8918-337f2ff9e3b8.html.

Wolf, Carissa, Peter Holley, and Wesley Lowery. "Armed Men, Led by Bundy Brothers, Take Over Federal Building in Oregon," *Washington Post,* January 3, 2016, https://www.washingtonpost.com/news/post-nation/wp/2016/01/03/armed-militia-bundy-brothers-take-over-federal-building-in-rural-oregon/.

Wolf, Zachary B. "Why Teacher Strikes are Touching Every Part of America," CNN, February 23, 2019. https://www.cnn.com/2019/02/23/politics/teacher-strikes-politics/index.html.

Workman, William D., Jr. *The Case for the South.* New York: Devin-Adair, 1960.

"World Is Seeing Injustices in Stores," *Charlotte (NC) Observer,* February 25, 1960.

Yan, Holly. "Here's What Teachers Accomplished with Their Protests This Year." CNN, May 29, 2018. https://www.cnn.com/2018/05/29/us/what-teachers-won-and-lost/index.html.

Zald, Mayer N. "Culture, Ideology, and Strategic Framing." In *Comparative Perspectives on Social Movements: Political Opportunities, Mobilizing Structures, and Cultural Framings,* edited by Doug McAdam, John D. McCarthy, and Mayer N. Zald, 261–74. New York: Cambridge University Press, 1996.

Zarefsky, David. "Four Senses of Rhetorical History," in *Doing Rhetorical History,* edited by Kathleen J. Turner, 19–32. Tuscaloosa: University of Alabama Press, 1998.

Zarefsky, David, and Victoria J. Gallagher. "From Constitutional 'Conflict' to 'Constitutional Question': Transformations in Early American Public Discourse." *Quarterly Journal of Speech* 76 (1990): 247–61.

Zimmerman, Samuel L. *Negroes in Greenville, 1970: An Exploratory Approach.* Greenville: South Carolina Tricentennial, 1970.

Contributors

RICHARD W. LEEMAN is Senior Associate Dean of the College of Arts and Sciences and professor of Communication Studies at the University of North Carolina at Charlotte. He is the author of *The Teleological Discourse of Barack Obama* (Lexington Books, 2012), coeditor (with Bernard K. Duffy) of *The Will of the People: A Critical Anthology of Great African American Speeches* (Southern Illinois University Press, 2012), and editor of *African American Orators: A Bio-Critical Sourcebook* (Greenwood Press, 1996). Leeman's PhD is from the University of Maryland.

SEAN PATRICK O'ROURKE is director of the Rhetoric Program, director of the Center for Speaking and Listening, and professor of Rhetoric and American Studies at Sewanee: The University of the South. He writes on rhetoric, rights, and protest, with a special interest in the period between 1948 and 1973. He is coeditor of two books, *Rhetoric, Race, Religion, and the Charleston Shootings: Was Blind but Now I See* (with Melody Lehn, Lexington Press, 2019) and *Like Wildfire: The Rhetoric of the Civil Rights Sit-Ins* (with Lesli K. Pace, University of South Carolina Press, 2020). O'Rourke holds JD and PhD degrees from the University of Oregon.

LESLI K. PACE is associate professor and chairperson of the Department of Communication Studies and Modern Languages at Southeast Missouri State University. Her research focus is on the rhetoric of gender and social movements. She has published articles in *Peace Studies Journal, Qualitative Inquiry,* and *Women and Language,* focusing on feminist ontology, women's movements, and parenting discourses. She is coeditor (with Sean Patrick O'Rourke) of *Like Wildfire: The Rhetoric of the Civil Rights Sit-Ins* (University of South Carolina Press, 2020). Pace's PhD is from Southern Illinois University.

STEPHEN SCHNEIDER is associate professor of English at the University of Louisville. He has published essays in *Technical Communication Quarterly, College English,* and *College Composition and Communication.* His first book, *You Can't Padlock an Idea: Rhetorical Education at the Highlander Folk School, 1932–1961,* was published by the University of South Carolina Press in 2014. Schneider has a PhD from Pennsylvania State University.

Index